Lewis Goldsmith

The Secret History of the Court and Cabinet of St. Cloud

Vol. 2

Lewis Goldsmith

The Secret History of the Court and Cabinet of St. Cloud
Vol. 2

ISBN/EAN: 9783337350253

Printed in Europe, USA, Canada, Australia, Japan

Cover: Foto ©ninafisch / pixelio.de

More available books at **www.hansebooks.com**

THE SECRET HISTORY

OF THE

COURT AND CABINET

OF

ST. CLOUD

IN A

SERIES OF LETTERS FROM A GENTLEMAN AT
PARIS TO A NOBLEMAN IN LONDON

WRITTEN DURING THE MONTHS OF

AUGUST, SEPTEMBER AND OCTOBER, 1805

IN TWO VOLUMES—VOLUME II

LONDON
H. S. NICHOLS & CO.
3 SOHO SQUARE AND 62A PICCADILLY W
MDCCCXCV

CONTENTS

Letter XLI

PAGE

Ill-temper of Bonaparte on his return from Milan From what arising—His violence and insolence to the Prussian and Saxon ambassadors. Restoration of ancient etiquette a desirable point to insist on from Bonaparte—His conduct to the army of England—Captain Fournois stabs himself on being struck by him—His proceedings in consequence. Discipline and spirit of the French troops—Instance of heroism in a private soldier. General Savary—His character, birth and employments 1

Letter XLII

The Bank of France ordered by Bonaparte to furnish him with a million and a half sterling at two hours' notice—Alarm of the public—Run upon the bank—Notes paid in copper coin—The people grow clamorous—Many arrested and transported to Cayenne—Total stagnation of trade—Some Jews offer to purchase the notes at discount—Are transported—Arrangements for resuming payment—Amount of notes in circulation at the time of stopping, and of specie in the bank—Shock given to its credit—Attempted to be supported by tyranny—Suspicion and severity of the police—Anecdotes 10

Letter XLIII

Rapacity and extortions of French officers in Hanover—Bribe Madame Bonaparte for their appointment. General Mortier—His birth—Military appointments—Mean addresses to Bonaparte—His marriage—His lady's gallantries—Splendid christening of his child—His wealth and character—A great favourite with Bonaparte.

Bernadotte—His birth, political intrigues, military exploits and violence—Sent ambassador to Vienna—His insolent conduct there—Bribed by Bonaparte on his assuming the imperial dignity—His barbarities and merciless extortions—His character . . 19

LETTER XLIV

Men of letters patronised by Bonaparte—Some obscure writers in England and Ireland pensioned by him — Literary mission to England intended—Bonaparte's liberal rewards to his panegyrists—Examples—Great number of works dedicated to him—More by Germans and Italians than by the French — Spanicetti and Ritterstein, genealogists of Bonaparte, magnificently rewarded by him—Vast number of pictures, statues and busts representing his person and exploits. Schumacher, a German artist, executes a model of a tomb for Bonaparte—How remunerated . 27

LETTER XLV

Misery and poverty of the French people—Wretchedness of the *ci-devant* nobles and returned emigrants—Their employments Anecdotes—Great number of suicides . . . 35

LETTER XLVI

Different opinions respecting Bonaparte's private character—Apparent attachment to his wife—His proposed divorce from her and marriage with a Russian princess—His intrigue with Mademoiselle George—Her insolent conduct. Chaptal—His former occupation—Political intrigues and employments—His wealth and character . 42

LETTER XLVII

Miserable state of Spain—Ignorance and presumption of the Prince of Peace—The Prince of Asturias endeavours to remove him—Receives a deputation from the Spanish nobles—Character of the Princess of Asturias. The Prince of Peace informed of their plans—His measures in consequence—Tries to conciliate the Prince and Princess Is repulsed. Character of Herman, secretary to the

French embassy in Spain—The Prince of Peace—His illiberal prejudices—Not liked by the French Government—Herman's intrigue with a girl in the suite of the Princess of Asturias—His discovery in consequence. Plan of the Prince and Princess—Disclosed by the French ambassador to the favourite—Consequent proceedings—The Duke of Montemar interferes—His speech to the King—Note of the Prince of Asturias to the King—Their reconciliation 48

Letter XLVIII

The Prince of Peace places spies round the Prince and Princess of Asturias—His insolent conduct to them—Indignation of the Spanish nobles—The history of Don Carlos written by order of the favourite—Burnt by the Queen's confessor—Dissimulation of the French ambassador, Beurnonville—Immense sums paid by Spain to France—Deranged state of the Spanish finances—Intrigue of Beurnonville to obtain a subsidy—The Prince and Princess of Asturias disavow his assertions—Punished in the persons of their favourites—Revolution and change of dynasty expected in Spain —Sovereignties intended for Bonaparte's brothers—Beurnonville's birth and character—His political and military employments . 58

Letter XLIX

Madame Bonaparte's fears of her brothers-in-law—Their powers during Napoleon's absence—His policy. Supposed consequence of Bonaparte's death. New military manners. General Liebeau —His birth, vulgarity, and character—Description of a military wedding. Colonel Frial—His birth and character—Disputes about their respective pretensions to the Imperial Crown among the military members of the party—A common subject of discussion and dispute among the military in general . 68

Letter L

Madame Chevalier—Her person and manners—Her early prostitution and first entrance on the stage—Her husband joins the Jacobin

CONTENTS

PAGE

Clubs, and is imprisoned as a terrorist — First appearance of Madame Chevalier on the Hamburg stage—Riot in consequence—Her gallantries and avarice—Employed by one of Talleyrand's female agents to go to Russia—Her intrigues with the Emperor Paul—Her cruelty and avarice—Procures the cruel treatment of the Sardinian Secretary—Number of her victims—Her insinuation, cunning and effrontery—Anecdotes. Female political incendiaries and intriguers sent by the French Government to Vienna, St. Petersburg and Berlin. Two ladies intended for the P—— of W—— and D—— of Y—— —Their persons and accomplishments . 80

Letter LI

Submission of America to the mandates of France—Views of France on the American Continent—Foments the disagreement between Spain and the United States—Captures and plunders American ships—Condemns all neutral ships trading with St. Domingo. General Turreaux, French ambassador to the United States—Discontented with President Jefferson—Why—Birth of Turreaux—His political intrigues and military exploits—Horrors committed by him in La Vendée—His letter to the National Convention—Arrested as a terrorist—Writes Memoirs of the Vendean war. Anecdote of Bonaparte. Wealth of Turreaux—His conceit and character 91

Letter LII

Discontent of Bonaparte's Italian subjects—Their miserable condition—Oppressed and plundered by French generals and governors. Menou—His birth and infamous character. Fate of the nobility who have joined the French Revolution. Melzi-Eril seduced by French philosophers—Approves of the French Revolution—Appointed vice-president of the Italian Republic—His chagrin on Bonaparte's assuming the sovereignty—Is refused leave to retire to Spain—Attempts suicide by poison . . 102

Letter LIII

The foreign ambassadors hesitate to salute Cambacérès and Le Brun Serene Highnesses—Bonaparte insists—They bribe Talleyrand,

CONTENTS xi

who obviates the difficulty. Cambacérès bribes Talleyrand, and is created a prince. Madame B——s, a female intriguer and tool of Talleyrand, alarms the Bavarian minister Cetto—He conducts this petty intrigue. Cambacérès—His birth—Infamous character—Raised to the consulate by Bonaparte—His wealth and titles—His brother . . 110

LETTER LIV

King of Sweden hated by Bonaparte—National character of the Swedes—Cause of Bonaparte's hatred—Baron Ehrensward constantly insulted by him—Orders issued to imprison the Baron for expressing his sentiments. Education and character of Baron Ehrensward. King of Sweden writes to Bonaparte on the seizure of the Duke of Enghien—Recalls Ehrensward, and orders a Court mourning. General Caulincourt and fifty banditti hired to seize the King of Sweden—Intentions of the French Government, if their plot had succeeded—Their plan to partition the Swedish territory. Character of the King of Sweden and his counsellors. D'Ehrenheim. Count de Fersen—His attachment and fidelity to the royal family of France—Refused admission to the Congress of Rastadt by Bonaparte. Baron d'Armfeldt—The friend of Gustavus III.—Appointed guardian of the present King—Sent ambassador to Italy—Outlawed—Takes refuge in Russia, and serves with distinction under Suwarow—Recalled to his country, and restored to his dignities—His military talents and spirit . . 116

LETTER LV

Bonaparte dreads the liberty of the Press—All foreign printers and booksellers under the control of his police—Emissaries employed to travel to collect literary intelligence—Number of French newspapers before and during the Revolution—Reduced by Bonaparte —Under the sole direction of Barrère—Foreign papers and publications prohibited under severe penalties. Examples of severity— Official presses established to forge foreign papers—Dangerous to question the veracity of the *Moniteur*—Anecdote . . . 124

LETTER LVI

Prince of Borghese—His birth—Joins the Revolution—His meanness and pride—Marries Madame Le Clerc's fortune—Her vices—Despises her husband—Her curious request to Bonaparte. Bonaparte exacts chastity from his sisters-in-law—Sudden disappearance of Princesses Joseph's and Louis' gallants. Princess Louis visits Madame Ney—A midnight occurrence during her stay—She is placed under the care of Madame Murat—Discovers a singular intrigue—Arrangement in consequence—Princess Louis' maids confined by the police—One of them pregnant by Louis . 130

LETTER LVII

Different sensations of the army of England on being ordered to march for Germany—Company of performers sent from Paris to amuse them—Plays and ballads written for the occasion—Great effect produced by them—"The Grenadier's Adieu," a ballad written by three authors—Profusely rewarded by Bonaparte. Stanzas on the rumour of a war with Austria—Distributed to the company at Madame Joseph's. Other poetasters—How rewarded. Curious blunder at Madame Talleyrand's. Anecdote of an ancient Tyrant 136

LETTER LVIII

Portugal forced from her neutrality by her connection with Spain—Portuguese plenipotentiary at Paris in 1797 imprisoned in the Temple—Extravagant demands of France on Portugal supported by the Prince of Peace—Unmerciful plunder of Portugal by France. General Lasnes—His birth—Former employments and infamous character—His mission to Portugal a punishment for robbing the military chest—His insolent manners at the Court of Lisbon—Smuggles—Quits his post and returns without apology Demands a change of ministry—Is recalled. General Junot His birth—Military appointments and exploits—His tyranny and corruption while Governor of Paris—His connection with a gang of robbers—Anecdote of his swindling. Fitte—His infamous character—Emigrates to England—Cheats the English Ministry—Procures the murder of his brother and sister . . . 145

Letter LIX

Impolicy of the League of 1793 in admitting any neutrality—Danger of neutral states. The late Count Bernstorf—His political character. The present Count Bernstorf—His system of politics not adapted to existing circumstances—Impolicy in changing the alliance of Russia for that of Prussia. Prince Royal of Denmark—His talents and character—Incapacity of his counsellors. A paragraph in the *Moniteur* disbands a Danish army—Neutrality of Denmark violated. Grouvelle, late French ambassador in Denmark—Protects and encourages Illuminati and innovators there—His education—Ingratitude to the Prince of Condé—His talents and vices. Daguesseau, his insignificant character—His secretary, Desaugiers, an incendiary 154

Letter LX

Avarice and rapacity of the Bonaparte family—Immense wealth of Napoleon—His imperial and royal palaces. Private châteaux of Madame Napoleon. Palaces and estates of Joseph, Lucien, Louis and Jerome—Of Madame Letitia Bonaparte, Princesses Baciocchi, Santa Cruce, Murat, Borghese—Of Cardinal Fesch—And other relatives of Bonaparte. Unparalleled revolution of property—Just cause of alarm to England . . . 160

Letter LXI

Daru pays an immense bribe for the place of Commissary-general to the French army in Germany—His great wealth acquired by gambling—The terror of all the gambling banks on the Continent. Extortions of the French generals in Germany. Augereau—His birth—Serves as a spy—As a common soldier, deserts—Is flogged—His infamy and crimes. Van Damme—His birth—Condemned to be hanged—Spared by the judge and sent to the galleys—His ingratitude—Disgraced by Moreau and Pichegru for his ferocity and crimes—Restored to rank by Bonaparte—His wealth . . 166

Letter LXII

Pillage and extortions of the French armies. General Ney, his conduct at Wetzlar—His birth—Former occupation—Political intrigues and military appointments—His wife, maid-of-honour to Empress Josephine—Her birth—Gallantries—Pleasing manners—Gambling and prostitution. Prince Murat, his crimes—Birth—Marries Bonaparte's sister—His immense wealth—Promotes and enriches his relations—Effect of his elevation on his father and mother. Rapine the chief object of revolutionists. Murat the executioner of Bonaparte's despotic and murderous commands—Jealous of his wife with her brother Lucien—Her coquetry and gallantries—Her favourite, Flahault . . . 171

Letter LXIII

Increased vigilance of the police at Paris since Bonaparte's departure for Germany—All mandates of arrest expedited by Louis Bonaparte His vicious character—A tragical intrigue—Another intrigue . 178

Letter LXIV

Dignified conduct of Russia, its able ministers. Count Woronzoff—His talents, services, and amiable character—Instance of his magnanimity. Prince Czartorinsky—His great information and polished manners. Count de Markoff—His political services—Exiled by Paul—Recalled by Alexander, and appointed ambassador to France—His surprise at the conduct of Bonaparte to foreign ambassadors—His witty letter to his Court on the occasion—His dignified conduct—Hated by Talleyrand. Talleyrand's low malice—Attempts to corrupt the fidelity of Madame Hus, the mistress of Count Markoff—Conversation of Count Markoff with him on the subject . 184

Letter LXV

Legion of Honour, when determined on—Distribution of arms of honour among the military—Creation of Knights—Members of the

CONTENTS xv

PAGE

Legion of Honour divided into classes Bonaparte's desire to have Sovereigns for members—Exchange of Orders between Bonaparte and the Kings of Spain and Prussia—Foreign Orders debased by being conferred on Cambacérès, Fouché, &c.—Grand officers of the Legion of Honour, *ci-devant* tailors, shoemakers, barbers, &c.; kings, electors and princes—Effect of the institution on the people—Villeaume, an engraver, forges letters of Knighthood, sells them and escapes—Baron von Rinken, the agent of a petty German Prince, confined in the Temple for offering patents of Knighthood for sale. Anecdotes of Captain Rouvais and a cobbler. Cambacérès reproved for partiality to the Prussian Eagle. Bonaparte ornamented with an immense number of Orders—Presented with the Grand Cross of Malta. Order of Confidence intended to be instituted by the Empress Josephine—Her mantle and star 192

LETTER LXVI

Fifteen persons brought prisoners from La Vendée—Their crime not known—What reported to be. Impolicy and cruelty of attempting to excite an insurrection in the Chouan departments. Apathy of the French people—The general poverty—Anecdote—Poverty of merchants and tradesmen—Vast number of speculators and bankruptcies—Numerous forgeries and swindling—Landholders burdened with taxes—Example Their spirit and independence . 200

LETTER LXVII

Military education of the French youth—The independence of Europe threatened by it—The only mode of averting the danger. Berthier's compliment to Bonaparte—The advantage of the French over their allies. Bad consequences of an education entirely military—Pointed out by Arnaud—His exile from Paris in consequence. Instance of severity against a schoolmaster for deviating from the established mode—His pupils taken care of by Government. Another instance of severity in this respect. New organisation of the Ministry of Police and number of spies increased . 207

LETTER LXVIII

The Pope's Nuncio publicly rebuked by Bonaparte. The relatives of Bonaparte's Great Officers generally appointed to the chief dignities of the Gallican Church—Their infamous characters. The brother of General Miollis—His notorious atheism and profligacy—Nominated by Bonaparte to the Bishopric of Digne—The Pope hesitates to grant a bull for that purpose—His Nuncio at Paris applies to Bonaparte—How answered—The nomination of Miollis confirmed by the Pope. Debauched character of the Italian bishops. Anecdotes of the Bishop of Pavia and of his grand vicars, Sarini and Rami. Hypocrisy of the French clergy—Anecdotes. Indifference of the French Government respecting the religious establishment — Want of Ministers — To what to be attributed—Bonaparte refuses the Pope to except the students in theology from the military conscription—Permits him to establish a seminary in the Ecclesiastical States . . 213

LETTER LXIX

Violation of the Prussian neutrality—Sudden alteration in the expressions of the French courtiers in regard to Prussia—Whence arising. Bonaparte's ascendancy in Prussia—Friendly intercourse between him and the King of Prussia, and the Empress Josephine and the Queen. Friendship of upstarts dangerous. Duroc's mission to Berlin—Its object—Followed by warlike preparations in Prussia—Necessity of Prussia's instantly joining the league against France. Reports of an alliance between Prussia and England. A war with Prussia desired in France—Why . . . 220

LETTER LXX

Instances of impolitic and degrading civility of the Prussian monarchs to the French. Field-marshal Knobelsdorff—His satirical reply to Siéyes. General Knobelsdorff—His insignificant character—Affection for Bonaparte—His favour with his Sovereign and political missions. Object of Count Haugwitz's mission to Vienna—Annual subsidy proposed by France to Prussia refused. Baron de Hardenberg—His political character—His talents Public employments—His private agents in foreign countries. Baron de Bülow—His singular person and manners—Confined in the Temple, and supported by Sir Sydney Smith. Marquis de Lucchesini—His character and political transactions. Marchioness de Lucchesini—Her manners and gallantries. Prince Baciocchi—His former occupation 225

LETTER LXXI

Unexampled cruelty of the French Government to Captain Wright. Necessity of regulating the distinction and treatment of prisoners of war Generous conduct of the English to the officers and men of French ships landing rebels in Scotland and Ireland, and malefactors in Wales. The firmness of Captain Wright offends the French Government—Riches and rank offered to him indignantly refused—He is put on the rack and most inhumanly tortured—His heroic conduct—Is placed under the care of a surgeon—New offers made him—Again racked—Undergoes the INFERNAL torments—Description of them—Strangled by a Mameluke. The particulars of this horrid transaction—How discovered—The release of Captain Wright promised to the Spanish ambassador—Why . . . 234

LETTER LXXII

Great changes to be made in the constitution and internal government of France, should Bonaparte return victorious — Heterogeneous composition of the tribunate and legislative corps. Carnot declaims against Bonaparte's imperial dignity, by his permission—His birth—Education and ingratitude to the House of Bourbon—His crimes and falsehood—His letter to Lebon—His talents and presumption—His wealth—Instance of his libertinism and cruelty—Despised and mistrusted by Bonaparte. Cavaignac—His former occupation—His revolutionary exploits—His atrocities Anecdotes. Pinet—His lust and cruelty . 240

CONTENTS

LETTER LXXIII

Vast naval schemes of Bonaparte—His immense resources—Great number of ships built since the present war. Malouet's official account of the number of officers and sailors—The conscripts universally prefer the naval to the military service. Genoa, an important naval station acquired by France—Number of ships building there and at Antwerp. Naples and Venice threatened —Deficiency of French Admirals. Murat appointed to the chief command of the combined fleets—The proposed plan of operations deranged by subsequent events. Admiral Truguet—His opinion of the French flotillas—Occasion of his disgrace—His character— Public employments—Hated by Talleyrand—Canes him publicly. Villeneuve—His naval exploits—His gasconade. Ganteaume— His promotions—Saves himself by swimming when *l'Orient* blew up at Aboukir—Letter of Bonaparte to him on the occasion —His naval exploits and character. La Crosse—His intrigues, fanaticism and cruelty . . . 247

LETTER LXXIV

Apathy of the French people—Indifferent about the victories obtained over the Austrians. Rejoicings at Madame Joseph Bonaparte's Patriotic verses and ballads—List of Bonaparte's intended kings, emperors, &c. Arthur O'Connor, his present rank and views in France. The Irish rebels universally despised—Treated as criminals, and act as such—Their infamy and ingratitude— Anecdote 254

LETTER LXXV

Absurdity and incoherence of the plan of the campaign of the Austrians. Inactivity of the army under the Archduke Charles— To what to be attributed—Character of the Archduke—His military life—Respected by his enemies—His proclamations composed with great adroitness. Massena—Deserts the army of his sovereign— Cause of his advancement in the French service—His military exploits and merciless pillage—Quarrels with Bonaparte—Appointed by him to the chief command in Italy His wealth and good fortune Disliked by the Bonapartes for his familiarity. Great talents of General St. Cyr His achievements. Count de Bellegarde His eminent services and distinguished talents . . 260

LETTER LXXVI

Bonaparte's insolent threat at Ulm against the Emperor of Germany — Conclusions to be drawn from it—Louis Bonaparte's public comment on it. Abbé Siéyes—His sanguinary plots and intrigues—Has betrayed and survived all factions—His restlessness and craft Cowardice and ambition — His wealth Talleyrand's opinion of him. Bonaparte's apparently indiscreet threat at Ulm accounted for. General Marmont His military education and public employments—His honourable character Bonaparte demands for him in marriage the daughter of the banker, Perregeaux Industry and ambition of Perregeaux—His public life and intrigue with Mademoiselle Mars. General Marmont's distinguished services —A great favourite of Bonaparte . . . 267

LETTER LXXVII

Another great Revolution supposed necessary to counterbalance that of France. Insignificance and presumption of General von Mack— His personal intrepidity at Lissa— His theoretical knowledge and declamation impose on the Emperor Joseph—His campaigns—His bad conduct at the head of the Neapolitan army—His pusillanimous conduct in the present campaign—His ill-health—His fidelity and honour . . . 276

THE SECRET HISTORY
OF THE
COURT AND CABINET
OF
ST. CLOUD

LETTER XLI

PARIS, *September*, 1805.

MY LORD,—Since my return here, I have never neglected to present myself before our Sovereign, on his days of grand reviews and grand diplomatic audiences. I never saw him more condescending, more agreeable, or, at least, less offensive, than on the day of his last levée, before he set out to be inaugurated a king of Italy; nor worse tempered, petulant, agitated, abrupt and rude than at his first grand audience after his arrival from Milan, when this ceremony had been performed. I am not the only one who made this remark; he did not disguise either his good or ill-humour; and it was only requisite to have eyes and ears to see and be disgusted at the difference of behaviour.

I have heard a female friend of Madame Bonaparte explain, in part, the cause of this alteration. Just before he set out for Italy, the agreeable news of the success of the first Rochefort squadron in the West Indies, and the escape of our Toulon fleet from the vigilance of your Lord Nelson, highly elevated his spirits, as it was the first naval enterprise of any consequence since his reign. I am certain that one grand naval victory would flatter his vanity and ambition more than all the glory of one of his most brilliant Continental campaigns. He had also, at that time, great expectations that another negotiation with Russia would keep the Continent submissive under his dictature, until he should find an opportunity of crushing your power. You may be sure that he had no small hopes of striking a blow in your country, after the junction of our fleet with the Spanish; not by any engagement between our Brest fleet and your Channel fleet, but under a supposition that you would detach squadrons to the East and West Indies in search of the combined fleet, which, by an unexpected return, according to orders, would have then left us masters of the Channel, and, if joined with the Batavian fleet, perhaps even of the North Sea. By the incomprehensible activity of Lord Nelson, and by the defeat (or, as we call it here, the negative victory) of Villeneuve and Gravina, all this first prospect had vanished. Our vengeance against a nation of shopkeepers we were not only under the necessity of postponing, but, from the unpolite threats and treaties of the Cabinet of St. Petersburg with those of Vienna and St. James', we were on the eve of a Continental war, and our gunboats, instead of being useful in carrying an army to the destruction of the tyrants of the seas, were burdensome, as an army was necessary to guard them, and to prevent these tyrants from capturing or destroying them. Such changes, in so short a period of time as three months, might irritate a temper less patient than that of Napoleon the First.

At his grand audience here, even after the army of England had moved towards Germany, when the die was cast, and his mind should, therefore, have been made up, he was almost insupportable. The low bows, and the still humbler expressions of the Prussian ambassador, the Marquis of Lucchesini, were hardly noticed; and the Saxon ambassador, Count de Buneau, was addressed in a language that no well-bred master ever uses in speaking to a menial servant. He did not cast a look, or utter a word, that was not an insult to the audience and a disgrace to his rank. I never before saw him vent his rage and disappointment so indiscriminately. We were, indeed (if I may use the term), humbled and trampled upon *en masse*. Some he put out of countenance by staring angrily at them; others he shocked by his hoarse voice and harsh words; and all — all of us — were afraid, in our turn, of experiencing something worse than our neighbours. I observed more than one minister, and more than one general, change colour, and even perspire, at His Majesty's approach.

I believe the members of the foreign diplomatic corps here will all agree with me, that, at a future congress, the restoration of the ancient and becoming etiquette of the kings of France would be as desirable a point to demand from the Emperor of the French as the restoration of the balance of power.

Before his army of England quitted its old quarters on the coast, the officers and men often felt the effects of his ungovernable temper. When several regiments of Grenadiers, of the division of Oudinot, were defiling before him on the 25th of last month, he frequently and severely, though without cause, reprobated their manner of marching, and once rode up to Captain Fournois, pushed him forwards with the point of a small cane, calling out, "*Sacré Dieu!* Advance; you walk like a turkey." In the first moment of indignation, the captain, striking at the cane with his sword, made a push, or a gesture, as if threatening the person of Bonaparte, who called out to his aide-de-camp, Savary, "Disarm the villain, and arrest him!"—"It is unnecessary," the captain replied; "I have served a tyrant, and merit my fate!" So saying, he passed his sword through his heart. His whole company stopped instantly, as at a word of command, and a general murmur was heard. "Lay down your arms, and march out of the file instantly," commanded Bonaparte, "or you shall be cut down for your mutiny by my Guides." They hesitated for a moment, but the Guides advancing to surround them, they obeyed, and were disarmed. On the following afternoon, by a special military commission, each tenth man was condemned to be shot; but Bonaparte pardoned them upon condition of serving for life in the colonies; and the whole company was ordered to the colonial dépôts. The widow and five children of Captain Fournois the next morning threw themselves at the Emperor's feet, presenting a petition, in which they stated that the pay of the captain had been their only support. "Well," replied Bonaparte to the kneeling petitioners, "Fournois was both a fool and a traitor; but, nevertheless, I will take care of you." Indeed, they have been so well taken care of that nobody knows what has become of them.

I am almost certain that I am not telling you what you did not know beforehand in informing you that the spirit of our troops is greatly different from that of the Germans, and even from that of your own country. Every one of our soldiers would prefer being shot to being beaten or caned. Flogging with us is out of the question. It may, perhaps, be national vanity, but I am doubtful whether any other army is, or can be, governed, with regard to discipline, in a less violent and more delicate manner, and, nevertheless, be kept in subordination, and perform the most brilliant exploits. Remember, I speak of our spirit of subordination and discipline, and not of our character as citizens, as patriots, or as subjects. I have often hinted it, but I believe I have not explained myself so fully before; but my firm opinion and persuasion is that, with regard to our loyalty, our duty, and our moral and political principles, another equally inconsistent and despicable people does not exist in the universe.

The condition of the slave is certainly in itself that of vileness; but is that slave a vile being who, for a blow, pierces his bosom because he is unable to avenge it? And what epithet can be given him who braves voluntarily a death seemingly certain, not from the love of his country, but from a principle of honour, almost incompatible with the dishonour of bondage?

During the siege of York Town, in America, we had, during one night, erected a battery, with intent to blow up

a place which, according to the report of our spies, was
your magazine of ammunition, &c. We had not time to
finish it before daylight; but one loaded twenty-four pounder
was mounted, and our cannoneer, the moment he was about
to fire it, was killed. Six more of our men, in the same
attempt, experienced the same fate. My regiment con-
stituted the advanced guard nearest to the spot, and La
Fayette brought me the order from the Commander-in-
Chief to engage some of my men upon that desperate
undertaking. I spoke to them, and two advanced, but
were both instantly shot by your sharp-shooters. I then
looked at my grenadiers, without uttering anything, when to
my sorrow one of my best and most orderly men advanced,
saying, "My colonel, permit me to try my fortune!"
Having assented, he went coldly amidst hundreds of bullets
whistling around his ears, set fire to the cannon, which
blew up a dépôt of powder, as was expected, and in
the confusion returned unhurt. La Fayette then presented
him with his purse. "No, sir," replied he, "money did
not make me venture upon such a perilous undertaking."
I understood my man, promoted him to a sergeant, and
recommended him to Rochambeau, who in some months
procured him the commission of a sub-lieutenant. He is
now one of Bonaparte's field-marshals, and the only one
of that rank who has no crimes to reproach himself with.

This man was the soldier of a despot; but was not his action that of a man of honour, which a staunch republican of ancient Rome would have been proud of? Who can explain this contradiction?

This anecdote about Fournois I heard General Savary relate at Madame Duchatel's, as a proof of Bonaparte's *generosity* and *clemency*, which, he affirmed, excited the admiration of the whole camp at Boulogne. I do not suppose this officer to be above thirty years of age, of which he has passed the first twenty-five in orphan-houses or in watch-houses; but no tyrant ever had a more cringing slave, or a more abject courtier. His affectation to extol everything that Bonaparte does, right or wrong, is at last become so habitual that it is naturalized, and you may mistake for sincerity that which is nothing but imposture or flattery.

This son of a Swiss porter is now one of Bonaparte's adjutants-general, a colonel of the Gendarmes d'Élite, a general of brigade in the army, and a commander of the Legion of Honour—all these places he owes, not to valour or merit, but to abjectness, immorality and servility. When an aide-de-camp with Bonaparte in Egypt, he served him as a spy on his comrades and on the officers of the staff, and was so much detested that, near Aboukir, several shots were fired at him in his tent by his own countrymen. He is supposed still to continue the same espionage; and as a colonel of the Gendarmes d'Élite, he is charged with the secret execution of all proscribed persons or state prisoners, who have been secretly condemned; a commission that a despot gives to a man he trusts, but dares not offer to a man he esteems. He is so well known that the instant he enters a society silence follows, and he has the whole conversation to himself. This he is stupid enough to take for a compliment, or for a mark of respect, or an acknowledgment of his superior parts and intelligence, when, in fact, it is a direct reproach with which prudence arms itself against suspected or known dishonesty. Besides his wife, he has to support six other women whom he has seduced and ruined; and, notwithstanding the numerous opportunities his master has procured him of pillaging and enriching himself, he is still much in debt; but woe to his creditors were they indiscreet enough to ask for their payments! The Secret Tribunal would soon seize them and transport them, or deliver them over to the hands of their debtor, to be shot as traitors or conspirators.

LETTER XLII

PARIS, *September*, 1805.

MY LORD,—I am told that it was the want of pecuniary resources that made Bonaparte so ill-tempered on his last levée day. He would not have come here at all, but preceded his army to Strasburg, had his minister of finances, Gaudin, and his minister of the public treasury, Marbois, been able to procure forty-four millions of livres £1,800,000—to pay a part of the arrears of the troops; and for the speedy conveyance of ammunition and artillery towards the Rhine.

Immediately after his arrival here, Bonaparte sent for the directors of the Bank of France, informing them that within twenty-four hours they *must* advance him thirty-six millions of livres—£1,500,000—upon the revenue of the last quarter of 1808. The president of the bank, Senator Garrat, demanded two hours to lay before the Emperor the situation of the bank, that His Majesty might judge what sum it was possible to spare without ruining the credit of an establishment hitherto so useful to the commerce of the empire. To this Bonaparte replied that he was not ignorant of the resources, or of the credit of the bank, any more than of its public utility; but that the affairs of state suffered from every hour's delay, and that, therefore, he insisted upon having the sum demanded even within two hours, partly in paper and partly in cash; and were they to show any more opposition, he would order the bank and all its effects to be seized that moment. The directors bowed and returned to the bank; whither they were followed by four waggons escorted by hussars, and belonging to the financial department of the army of England. In these were placed eight millions of livres in cash; and twenty-eight millions in bank-notes were delivered to M. Lefévre, the secretary-general of Marbois, who presented, in exchange, Bonaparte's bond and security for the amount, bearing an interest of five per cent. yearly.

When this money transaction was known to the public, the alarm became general, and long before the hour the bank usually opens the adjoining streets were crowded with persons desiring to exchange their notes for cash. During the night the directors had taken care to pay themselves for the bank-notes in their own possession with silver or gold, and, as they expected a run, they ordered all persons to be paid in copper coin, as long as any money of this metal remained. It required a long time to count those halfpennies and centimes (five of which make a sou, or halfpenny), but the people were not tired with waiting until towards three o'clock in the afternoon, when the bank is shut up. They then became so clamorous that a company of gendarmes was placed for protection at the entrance of the bank; but, as the tumult increased, the street was surrounded by the police guards, and above six hundred individuals, many of them women, were carried, under an escort, to different police commissaries, and to the prefecture of the police. There most of them, after being examined, were reprimanded and released. The same night, the police spies reported in the coffee-houses of the Palais Royal, and on the Boulevards, that this run on the bank was encouraged, and paid for, by English emissaries, some of whom were already taken, and would be executed on the next day. In the morning, however, the streets adjoining the bank were still more crowded, and the crowd still more tumultuous, because payment was refused for all notes but those of five hundred livres £21. The activity of the police agents, supported by the gendarmes and police soldiers, again restored order, after several hundred persons had been again taken up for their mutinous conduct. Of these many were, on the same evening, loaded with chains, and, placed in carts under military escort, paraded about near the bank and the Palais Royal; the police having, as a measure of safety, under suspicion that they were influenced by British gold, condemned them to be transported to Cayenne; and the carts set out on the same night for Rochefort, the place of their embarkation.

On the following day, not an individual approached the bank, but all trade and all payments were at a stand: nobody would sell but for ready money, and nobody who had bank-notes would part with cash. Some Jews and money-brokers in the Palais Royal offered cash for these bills, at a discount of from ten to twenty per cent. But these usurers were, in their turn, taken up and transported, as agents of Pitt. An interview was then demanded by the directors and principal bankers with the ministers of finance and of the public treasury. In this conference it was settled that, as soon as the two millions of dollars on their way from Spain had arrived at Paris, the bank should reassume its payments. These dollars Government would lend the bank for three months, and take in return its notes, but the bank was, nevertheless, to pay an interest of six per cent. during that period. All the bankers agreed not to press unnecessarily for any exchange of bills into cash, and to keep up the credit of the bank even by the individual credit of their own houses.

You know, I suppose, that the Bank of France has never issued but two sorts of notes; those of one thousand livres—£42 and those of five hundred livres—£21. At the day of its stoppage, sixty millions of livres— £2,500,000 —of the former, and fifteen millions of livres—£625,000— of the latter, were in circulation ; and I have heard a banker assert that the bank had not then six millions of livres—£250,000—in money and bullion, to satisfy the claims of its creditors, or to honour its bills.

The shock given to the credit of the bank by this last requisition of Bonaparte will be felt for a long time, and will with difficulty ever be repaired under his despotic government. Even now, when the bank pays in cash, our merchants make a difference from five to ten per cent. between purchasing for specie or paying in bank-notes ; and this mistrust will not be lessened hereafter. You may, perhaps, object that, as long as the bank pays, it is absurd for anyone possessing its bills to pay dearer than with cash, which might so easily be obtained. This objection would stand with regard to your, or any other free country, but here, where no payments are made in gold, but always in silver or copper, it requires a cart to carry away forty, thirty, or twenty thousand livres, in coin of these metals, and would immediately excite suspicion that a bearer of these bills was an emissary of our enemies, or an enemy of our Government. With us, unfortunately, suspicion is the same as conviction, and chastisement follows it as its shadow.

A manufacturer of the name of Debrais, established in the Rue St. Martin, where he had for years carried on business in the woollen line, went to the bank two days after it had begun to pay. He demanded, and obtained, exchange for twenty-four thousand livres—£1,000 in notes, necessary for him to pay what was due by him to his workmen. The same afternoon six of our custom-house officers, accompanied by police agents and gendarmes, paid him a domiciliary visit under pretence of searching for English goods. Several bales were seized as being of that description, and Debrais was carried a prisoner to La Forcé. On being examined by Fouché, he offered to prove, by the very men who had fabricated the suspected goods, that they were not English. The minister silenced him by saying that Government had not only evidence of the contrary, but was convinced that he was employed as an English agent to hurt the credit of the bank, and therefore, if he did not give up his accomplices or employers, had condemned him to transportation. In vain did his wife and daughters petition to Madame Bonaparte; Debrais is now at Rochefort, if not already embarked for our colonies.

When he was arrested, a seal, as usual, was put on his house, from which his wife and family were turned out, until the police should have time to take an inventory of his effects, and had decided on his fate. When Madame Debrais, after much trouble and many pecuniary sacrifices, at last obtained permission to have the seals removed, and re-enter her house, she found that all her plate and more than half her goods and furniture had been stolen and carried away. Upon her complaint of this theft she was thrown into prison for not being able to support her complaint with proofs, and for attempting to vilify the characters of the agents of our Government. She is still in prison, but her daughters are by her orders disposing of the remainder of their parents' property, and intend to join their father as soon as their mother has recovered her liberty.

The same tyranny that supports the credit of our bank also keeps up the price of our stocks. Any of our great stockholders who sell out to any large amount, if they are unable to account for, or unwilling to declare the manner in which they intend to employ, their money, are immediately arrested, sometimes transported to the colonies, but more frequently exiled into the country, to remain under the inspection of some police agent, and are not allowed to return here without the previous permission of our Government. Those of them who are upstarts, and have made their fortune since the Revolution by plunder, or as contractors, are still more severely treated, and are often obliged to renounce part of their ill-gotten wealth to save the remainder, or to preserve their liberty or lives. A revisal of their former accounts, or an inspection of their past transactions, is a certain and efficacious threat to keep them in silent submission, as they all well understand the meaning of them.

Even foreigners, whom our numerous national bankruptcies have not yet disheartened, are subject to these measures of rigour or vigour requisite to preserve our public credit. In the autumn of last year a Dutchman of the name of Van der Winkel sold out by his agent for three millions of livres £125,000—in our stock on one day, for which he bought up bills upon Hamburg and London. He lodged in the Hôtel des Quatre Nations, Rue Grenelle, where the landlord, who is a *patriot*, introduced some police agents into his apartments during his absence. These broke open all his trunks, drawers, and even his writing-desk, and when he entered, seized his person, and carried him to the Temple. By his correspondence it was discovered that all this money was to be brought over to England: a reason more than sufficient to incur the suspicion of our Government. Van der Winkel spoke very little French, and he continued, therefore, in confinement three weeks before he was examined, as our secret police had not at Paris any of its agents who spoke Dutch. Carried before Fouché, he avowed that the money was destined for England, there to pay for some plantations which he desired to purchase in Surinam and Barbice. His interpreter advised him, by the orders of Fouché, to alter his mind, and, as he was fond of colonial property, lay out his money in plantations at Cayenne, which was in the vicinity of Surinam, and where Government would recommend him advantageous purchases. It was hinted to him, also, that this was a particular favour, and a proof of the generosity of our Government, as his papers contained many matters that might easily be construed to be of a treasonable nature. After consulting with Schimmelpenninck, the ambassador of his country, he wrote for his wife and children, and was seen safe with them to Bordeaux by our police agents, who had hired an American vessel to carry them all to Cayenne. This certainly is a new method to populate our colonies with capitalists.

LETTER XLIII

Paris, *September*, 1805.

My Lord,—Hanover has been a mine of gold to our Government, to its generals, to its commissaries, and to its favourites. According to the boasts of Talleyrand, and the avowal of Berthier, we have drawn from it within two years more wealth than has been paid in contributions to the Electors of Hanover for this century past, and more than half-a-century of peace can restore to that unfortunate country. It is reported here that each person employed in a situation to make his fortune in the Continental States of the King of England (a name given here to Hanover in courtesy to Bonaparte) was laid under contribution, and expected to make certain douceurs to Madame Bonaparte; and it is said that she has received from Mortier three hundred thousand livres, and from Bernadotte two hundred and fifty thousand livres, besides other large sums from our military commissaries, treasurers, and other agents in the Electorate.

General Mortier is one of the few favourite officers of

Bonaparte who have distinguished themselves under his rivals, Pichegru and Moreau, without ever serving under him. Edward Adolph Casimer Mortier is the son of a shopkeeper, and was born at Cambray in 1768. He was a shopman with his father until 1791, when he obtained a commission, first as a lieutenant of carabiniers, and afterwards as captain of the first battalion of volunteers of the Department of the North. His first sight of an enemy was on the 30th of April, 1792, near Quievrain, where he had a horse killed under him. He was present in the battles of Jemappes, of Nerwinde, and of Pellenberg. At the battle of Houdscoote he distinguished himself so much as to be promoted to an adjutant-general. He was wounded at the battle of Fleurus, and again at the passage of the Rhine, in 1795, under General Moreau. During 1796 and 1797 he continued to serve in Germany, but in 1798 and 1799 he headed a division in Switzerland, from which Bonaparte recalled him, in 1800, to command the troops in the capital and its environs. His address to Bonaparte, announcing the votes of the troops under him respecting the consulate for life, and the elevation to the imperial throne, contain such mean and abject flattery, that, for a true soldier, it must have required more self-command and more courage to pronounce them than to brave the fire of a hundred cannons; but these very addresses, contemptible as their contents are, procured him the field-marshal's staff. Mortier well knew his man, and that his cringing in ante-chambers would be better rewarded than his services in the field. I was not present when Mortier spoke so shamefully, but I have heard, from persons who witnessed this farce, that he had his eyes fixed on the ground the whole time, as if to say, "I grant that I speak as a despicable being, and I grant that I am so; but what shall I do, tormented as I am by ambition to figure among the great, and to riot among the wealthy? Have compassion on my weakness, or, if you have not, I will console myself with the idea that my meanness is only of the duration of half-an-hour, while its recompense—my rank—will be permanent."

Mortier married, in 1799, the daughter of the landlord of the Belle Sauvage inn at Coblentz, who was pregnant by him, or by some other guest of her father. She is pretty, but not handsome, and she takes advantage of her husband's *complaisance* to console herself both for his absence and infidelities. When she was delivered of her last child, Mortier positively declared that he had not slept with her for twelve months, and the babe has, indeed, less resemblance to him than to his valet de chambre. The child was baptised with great splendour; the Emperor and the Empress were the sponsors, and it was christened by Cardinal Fesch. Bonaparte presented Madame Mortier on this occasion with a diamond necklace, valued at one hundred and fifty thousand livres—£6,000.

During his different campaigns, and particularly during his glorious campaign in Hanover, he has collected property to the amount of seven millions of livres, laid out in estates and lands. He is considered by other generals as a brave captain, but an indifferent chief; and among our fashionables and our courtiers he is held up as a model of connubial fidelity—satisfying himself with keeping three mistresses only.

There was no truth in the report that his recall from Hanover was in consequence of any disgrace: on the contrary, it was a new proof of Bonaparte's confidence and attachment. He was recalled to take the command of the artillery of Bonaparte's household troops the moment Pichegru, George and Moreau were arrested, and when the imperial title had been resolved on. More resistance against this innovation was at that time expected than experienced.

Bernadotte, who succeeded Mortier in the command of our army in Hanover, is a man of a different stamp. His father was a chair-man, and he was born at Paris in 1763. In 1779 he enlisted in the regiment called *La Vieille Marine*, where the Revolution found him a serjeant. This regiment was then quartered at Toulon, and the emissaries of anarchy and licentiousness engaged him as one of their agents. His activity soon destroyed all discipline, and the troops, instead of attending to their military duty, followed him to the debates and discussions of the Jacobin clubs. Being arrested and ordered to be tried for his mutinous, scandalous behaviour, an insurrection liberated him, and forced his accusers to save their lives by flight. In April, 1790, he headed the banditti who murdered the governor of the Fort St. Jean at Marseilles, and who afterwards occasioned the civil war in Comtat Venaigin, where he served under Jourdan, known by the name of *Coup-tell*, or cut-throat, who made him a colonel and his aide-de-camp. In 1794 he was employed, as a general of brigade, in the army of the Sambre and Meuse : and, during the campaigns of 1795 and 1796, he served under another Jourdan, the general, without much distinction ; except that he was accused by him of being the cause of all the disasters of the last campaign, by the complete rout he suffered near Neumark on the 23rd of August, 1796. His division was ordered to Italy in 1797, where, against the laws of nations, he arrested M. d'Antraigues, who was attached to the Russian legation. When the Russian ambassador tried to dissuade him from committing this injustice, and this violation of the rights of privileged persons, he replied. "There is no question here of any other right or justice than the right and justice of power, and I am here the strongest. M. d'Antraigues is our enemy; were he victorious, he would cause us all to be shot. I repeat, I am here the strongest, *et nous verrons.*"

After the Peace of Campo Formio, Bernadotte was sent as an ambassador to the Court of Vienna, accompanied by a numerous escort of Jacobin propagators. Having procured the liberty of Austrian *patriots*, whose lives, forfeit to the law, the lenity of the Cabinet of Vienna had spared, he thought that he might attempt anything; and, therefore, on the anniversary day of the fête for the levy *en masse* of the inhabitants of the capital, he insulted the feelings of the loyal, and excited the discontented to rebellion, by placing over the door and in the windows of his house the tricoloured flags. This outrage the Emperor was unable to prevent his subjects from resenting. Bernadotte's house was invaded, his furniture broken to pieces, and he was forced to save himself at the house of the Spanish ambassador. As a satisfaction for this attack, provoked by his own insolence, he demanded the immediate dismissal of the Austrian minister, Baron Thugut, and threatened, in case of refusal, to leave Vienna, which he did on the next day. So disgraceful was his conduct regarded, even by the Directory, that this event made but little impression, and no alteration in the continuance of their intercourse with the Austrian Government.

In 1799, he was for some weeks a minister of the war department, from which his incapacity caused him to be dismissed. When Bonaparte intended to seize the reins of State, he consulted Bernadotte, who spoke as an implacable Jacobin until a douceur of three hundred thousand livres—£12,000—calmed him a little, and convinced him that the Jacobins were not infallible or their government the best of all possible governments. In 1801, he was made the commander-in-chief in the Western Department, where he exercised the greatest barbarities against the inhabitants, whom he accused of being still chouans and royalists.

With Augereau and Massena, Bernadotte is a merciless plunderer. In the summer, 1796, he summoned the magistrates of the free and neutral city of Nuremberg to bring him, under pain of military execution, within twenty-four hours, two millions of livres—£84,000. With much difficulty this sum was collected. The day after he had received it, he insisted upon another sum to the same amount within another twenty-four hours, menacing in case of disobedience to give the city up to a general pillage by his troops. Fortunately, a column of Austrians advanced and delivered them from the execution of his threats. The troops under him were, both in Italy and in Germany, the terror of the inhabitants, and when defeated were, from their pillage and murder, hunted like wild beasts. Bernadotte has by these means within ten years become master of a fortune of ten millions of livres —£420,000.

Many have considered Bernadotte a revolutionary fanatic, but they are in the wrong. Money engaged him in the cause of the Revolution, where the first crimes he had perpetrated fixed him. The many massacres under Jourdan the cutthroat, committed by him in the Court at Venaigin, no doubt display a most sanguinary character. A lady, however, in whose house in La Vendée he was quartered six months, has assured me that, to judge from his conversation, he is not naturally cruel, but that his imagination is continually tormented with the fear of gibbets which he knows that his crimes have merited, and that, therefore, when he stabs others, he thinks it commanded by the necessity of preventing others from stabbing him. Were he sure of impunity, he would perhaps show humanity as well as justice. Bernadotte is not only a grand officer of the Legion of Honour, but *a Knight of the Royal Prussian Order of the Black Eagle.*

LETTER XLIV

Paris, *September*, 1805.

My Lord,— Bonaparte has taken advantage of the remark of Voltaire, in his "Life of Louis XIV.," that this Prince owed much of his celebrity to the well-distributed pensions among men of letters in France and in foreign countries. According to a list shown me by Fontanes, the president of the legislative corps and a director of literary pensions, even in your country and in Ireland he has nine literary pensioners. Though the names of your principal authors and men of letters are not unknown to me, I have never read nor heard of any of those I saw in the list, except two or three as editors of some newspapers, magazines, or trifling and scurrilous party pamphlets. I made this observation to Fontanes, who replied that these men, though obscure, had, during the last peace, been very useful, and would be still more so after another pacification ; and that Bonaparte must be satisfied with these until he could gain over men of greater talents. He granted also that men of true genius and literary eminence were, in England, more careful of the dignity of their character than those of Germany and Italy, and more difficult to be bought over. He added that, as soon as the war ceased, he should cross the Channel on a literary mission, from which he hoped to derive more success than from that which was undertaken three years ago by Fiévée.

To these men of letters, who are themselves, with their writings, devoted to Bonaparte, he certainly is very liberal. Some he has made tribunes, prefects, or legislators; others he has appointed his ministers in foreign countries, and on those to whom he has not yet been able to give places, he bestows much greater pensions than any former sovereign of this country allowed to a Corneille, a Racine, a Boileau, a Voltaire, a Crebillon, a d'Alembert, a Marmontel, and other heroes of our literature and honours to our nation. This liberality is often carried too far, and thrown away upon worthless subjects, whose very flattery displays absence of taste and genius, as well as of modesty and shame. To a fellow of the name of Dagée, who sang the coronation of Napoleon the First in two hundred of the most disgusting and ill-digested lines that ever were written, containing neither metre nor sense, was assigned a place in the administration of the forest department, worth twelve thousand livres in the year £500 besides a present, in ready money, of one hundred napoléons d'or. Another poetaster, Barré, who has served and sung the chiefs of all former factions, received for an ode of forty lines on Bonaparte's birthday, an office at Milan, worth twenty thousand livres in the year—£840—and one hundred napoléons d'or for his travelling expenses.

The sums of money distributed yearly by Bonaparte's agents for dedications to him by French and foreign authors, are still greater than those fixed for regular literary pensions. Instead of discouraging these foolish and impertinent contributions, which genius, ingenuity, necessity or intrusion, lay on his vanity, he rather encourages them. His name is, therefore, found in more dedications published within these last five years than those of all other sovereign princes of Europe taken together for this last century. In a man whose name, unfortunately for humanity, must always live in history, it is a childish and unpardonable weakness to pay so profusely for the short and uncertain *immortality* which some dull or obscure scribbler or poetaster confers on him.

During the last Christmas holidays I dined at Madame Remisatu's, in company with Duroc. The question turned upon literary productions and the comparative merit of the compositions of modern French and foreign authors. "As to the merits or the quality," said Duroc, "I will not take upon me to judge, as I profess myself totally incompetent; but as to their size and quantity I have tolerably good information, and it will not, therefore, be very improper in me to deliver my opinion. I am convinced that the German and Italian authors are more numerous than those of my own country, for the following reasons. I suppose, from what I have witnessed and experienced for some years past, that of every book or publication printed in France, Italy and Germany, each tenth is dedicated to the Emperor. Now, since last Christmas ninety-six German and seventy-one Italian authors have inscribed their works to His Majesty, and been rewarded for it; while during the same period only sixty-six Frenchmen have presented their offerings to their Sovereign." For my part I think Duroc's conclusion tolerably just.

Among all the numerous hordes of authors who have been paid, recompensed, or encouraged by Bonaparte, none have experienced his munificence more than the Italian Spanicetti and the German Ritterstein. The former presented him a genealogical table, in which he *proved* that the Bonaparte family, before their emigration from Tuscany to Corsica, four hundred years ago, were allied to the most ancient Tuscany families, even to that of the House of Medicis; and as this house has given two queens to the Bourbons when sovereigns of France, the Bonapartes are therefore relatives of the Bourbons; and the sceptre of the French empire is still *in the same family*, though *in a more worthy branch*. Spanicetti received one thousand louis d'or − £1,000—in gold, a pension of six thousand livres £250 for life, and the place of a *chef du bureau* in the ministry of the home department of the kingdom of Italy, producing eighteen thousand livres yearly— £750.

Ritterstein, a Bavarian genealogist, *proved* the pedigree of the Bonapartes as far back as the first crusades, and that the name of the friend of Richard Cœur de Lion was not Blondel, but Bonaparte; that he exchanged the latter for the former only to marry into the Plantagenet family, the last branch of which has since been extinguished by its intermarriage and incorporation with the House of Stuart, and that, therefore, Napoleon Bonaparte is not only related to most sovereign princes of Europe, but has more right to the throne of Great Britain than George the Third, being descended from the male branch of the Stuarts; while this prince is only descended from the female branch of the same royal house. Ritterstein was presented with a snuff-box with Bonaparte's portrait set with diamonds, valued at twelve thousand livres, and received twenty-four thousand livres ready money, together with a pension of nine thousand livres —£375—in the year until he could be better provided for. He was, besides, nominated a Knight of the Legion of Honour. It cannot be denied but that Bonaparte rewards like a real Emperor.

But artists as well as authors obtain from him the same encouragement, and experience the same liberality. In our different museums we, therefore, already see and admire upwards of two hundred pictures, representing the different actions, scenes, and achievements of Bonaparte's public life. It is true they are not all highly finished or well composed or delineated, but they all strike the spectators more or less with surprise or admiration: and it is with us, as I suppose with you, and everywhere else, the multitude decide: for one competent judge or real connoisseur, hundreds pass, who stare, gape, are charmed, and inspire thousands of their acquaintance, friends and neighbours with their own satisfaction. Believe me, Napoleon the First well knows the age, his contemporaries, and, I fear, even posterity.

That statuaries and sculptors consider him also as a generous patron, the numerous productions of their chisels in France, Italy and Germany, having him for their object, seem to evince. Ten sculptors have already represented his passage over the Mount St. Bernard, eighteen his passage over Pont de Lodi, and twenty-two that over Pont d'Arcole. At Rome, Milan, Turin, Lyons and Paris are statues of him representing his natural size: and our ten thousand municipalities have each one of his busts: without mentioning the thousands of busts all over Europe, not excepting even your own country. When Bonaparte sees under the windows of the Tuileries the statue of Caesar placed in the garden of that palace, he cannot help saying to himself, "Marble lives longer than man." Have you any doubt that his ambition and vanity extend beyond the grave?

The only artist I ever heard of who was disappointed and unrewarded for his labour in attempting to *eternize* the memory of Napoleon Bonaparte, was a German of the name of Schumacher. It is, indeed, allowed that he was more industrious, able, and well-meaning than ingenious or considerate. He did not consider that it would be no compliment to give the *immortal* hero a hint of being a *mortal* man. Schumacher had employed near three years in planning and executing in marble the prettiest model of a sepulchral monument I have ever seen, read or heard of. He had inscribed it, "*The Future Tomb of Bonaparte the Great.*" Under the patronage of Count de Beust, he arrived here; and I saw the model in the house of this minister of the German Elector Arch-Chancellor, where also many French artists went to inspect it. Count de Beust asked de Segur, the grand master of the ceremonies, to request the Emperor to grant Schumacher the honour of showing him his performance. De Segur advised him to address himself to Duroc, who referred him to Denon, who, after looking at it, could not help paying a just tribute to the execution and to the talents of the artist, though he disapproved of the subject, and declined mentioning it to the Emperor. After three months' attendance in this capital, and all petitions and memorials to our great folks remaining unanswered, Schumacher obtained an audience of Fouché, in which he asked permission to exhibit his model of Bonaparte's tomb to the public for money, so as to be enabled to return to his country. "Where is it now?" asked Fouché.—"At the minister's of the Elector Arch-Chancellor," answered the artist. — "But where do you intend to show it for money?" continued Fouché.—"In the Palais Royal."—"Well, bring it there," replied Fouché. The same evening that it was brought there, Schumacher was arrested by a police commissary, his model packed up, and, with himself, put under the care of two gendarmes, who carried them both to the other side of the Rhine. Here the Elector of Baden gave him some money to return to his home, near Aschaffenburg, where he has since exposed for money the model of a *grand* tomb for a *little* man. I have just heard that one of your countrymen has purchased it for one hundred and fifty louis d'or.

LETTER XLV

Paris, *September*, 1805.

My Lord,—Those who only are informed of the pageantry of our Court, of the expenses of our courtiers, of the profusion of our Emperor, and of the immense wealth of his family and favourites, may easily be led to believe that France is one of the happiest and most prosperous countries in Europe. But for those who walk in our streets, who visit our hospitals, who count the number of beggars and of suicides, of orphans and of criminals, of prisoners and of executioners, it is a painful necessity to reverse the picture, and to avow that nowhere comparatively can there be found so much collective misery. And it is not here, as in other states, that these unfortunate, reduced or guilty are persons of the lowest classes of society; on the contrary, many, and, I fear, the far greater part, appertain to the *ci-devant* privileged classes, descended from ancestors noble, respectable and wealthy, but who by the Revolution have been degraded to misery or infamy, and perhaps to both.

When you stop but for a moment in our streets to look at something exposed for sale in a shop-window, or for any other cause of curiosity or want, persons of both sexes, decently dressed, approach you, and whisper to you: " Sir, bestow your charity on the Marquis, or Marchioness —on the Baron, or Baroness, such a one, ruined by the Revolution ": and you sometimes hear names on which history has shed so brilliant a lustre, that, while you contemplate the deplorable reverse of human greatness, you are not a little surprised to find that it is in your power to relieve with a trifle the wants of the grandson of an illustrious warrior, before whom nations trembled, or of the granddaughter of that eminent statesman who often had in his hands the destiny of empires. Some few solitary walks, *incognito*, by Bonaparte, in the streets of his capital, would perhaps be the best preservative against unbounded ambition and confident success that philosophy could present to unfeeling tyranny.

Some author has written that "want is the parent of industry, and wretchedness the mother of ingenuity." I know that you have often approved and rewarded the ingenious productions of my emigrated countrymen in England; but here their labours and their endeavours are disregarded; and if they cannot or will not produce anything to flatter the pride or appetite of the powerful or rich upstarts, they have no other choice left but beggary or crime, meanness or suicide. How many have I heard repent of ever returning to a country where they have no expectation of justice in their claims, no hope of relief in their necessities, where death by hunger, or by their own hands, is the final prospect of all their sufferings.

Many of our ballad-singers are disguised emigrants; and I know a *ci-devant* marquis who is, *incognito*, a groom to a contractor, the son of his uncle's porter. Our old pedlars complain that their trade is ruined by the counts, by the barons and chevaliers who have monopolized all their business. Those who pretend to more *dignity*, but who have in fact less honesty, are employed in our billiard and gambling-houses. I have seen two music-grinders, one of whom was formerly a captain of infantry, and the other a counsellor of parliament. Every day you may bestow your penny or halfpenny on two veiled girls playing on the guitar or harp—the one the daughter of a *ci-devant* duke, and the other of a *ci-devant* marquis, a general under Louis XVI. They are usually placed, the one on the Boulevards, and the other in the Elysian Fields; each with an old woman by her side, holding a begging-box in her hand. I am told one of the women has been the nurse of one of those ladies. What a recollection, if she thinks of the past, in contemplating the present!

On the day of Bonaparte's coronation, and a little before he set out with his Pope and other splendid retinue, an old man was walking slowly on the Quai de Voltaire, without saying a word, but a label was pinned to his hat with this inscription: "*I had sixty thousand livres rent—* [£2,500]*—I am eighty years of age, and I request alms.*" Many individuals, even some of Bonaparte's soldiers, gave him their mite; but as soon as he was observed he was seized by the police agents, and has not since been heard of. I am told his name is De la Roche, a *ci-devant Chevalier de St. Louis*, whose property was sold in 1793 as belonging to an emigrant, though at the time he was shut up here as a prisoner, suspected of aristocracy. He has since for some years been a water-carrier; but his strength failing, he supported himself lately entirely by begging. The value of the dress of one of Bonaparte's running footmen might have been sufficient to relieve him for the probably short remainder of his days. But it is more easy and agreeable in this country to bury undeserved want in dungeons than to renounce unnecessary and useless show to relieve it. In the evening the remembrance of these sixty thousand livres of the poor Chevalier deprived me of all pleasure in beholding the sixty thousand lamps decorating and illuminating Bonaparte's palace of the Tuileries.

Some of the emigrants, whose strength of body age

has not impaired, or whose vigour of mind misfortunes have not depressed, are now serving as officers or soldiers under the Emperor of the French, after having for years fought in vain for the cause of a king of France in the brave army of Condé. Several are even doing duty in Bonaparte's household troops, where I know one who is a captain, and who, for distinguishing himself in combating the republicans, received the Order of St. Louis, but is now made a knight of Napoleon's Republican Order, the Legion of Honour, for *bowing* gracefully to Her Imperial Majesty the Empress. As he is a man of real honour, this favour is not quite in its place; but I am convinced that should one day an opportunity present itself, he will not miss it, but prove that he has never been misplaced. Another emigrant who, after being a page to the Duke of Angoulême, made four campaigns as an officer of the Uhlans in the service of the Emperor of Germany, and was rewarded with the Military Order of Maria Theresa, is now a knight of the Legion of Honour, and an officer of the Mamelukes of the Emperor of the French. Four more emigrants have engaged themselves in the same corps as *common Mamelukes*, after being for seven years volunteers in the legion of Mirabeau, under the Prince de Condé. It were to be wished that the whole of this favourite corps were composed of returned emigrants. I am sure they would never betray the confidence of Napoleon, but they would also never swear allegiance to another Bonaparte.

While the humbled remnants of one sex of the *ci-devant* privileged classes are thus or worse employed, many persons of the other sex have preferred domestic servitude to courtly splendour, and are chambermaids or governesses, when they might have been maids-of-honour or ladies-in-waiting. Mademoiselle de R——, daughter of Marquis de R.——, was offered a place as a maid-of-honour to Princess Murat, which she declined, but accepted at the same time the offer of being a companion of the rich Madame Moulin, whose husband is a *ci-devant* valet of Count de Brienne. Her father and brother suffered for this choice and preference, which highly offended Bonaparte, who ordered them both to be transported to Guadeloupe, under pretence that the latter had said in a coffee-house that his sister would rather have been the housemaid of the wife of a *ci-devant* valet, than the friend of the wife of a *ci-devant* assassin and Septembrizer. It was only by a valuable present to Madame Bonaparte from Madame Moulin, that Mademoiselle de R—— was not included in the act of proscription against her father and brother.

I am sorry to say that returned emigrants have also been arrested for frauds and debts, and even tried and convicted of crimes. But they are proportionally few, compared with those who, without support, and perhaps without hope, and from want of resignation and submission to the will of Providence, have in despair had recourse to the pistol or dagger, or in the River Seine buried their remembrance both of what they have been and of what they were. The suicides of this vicious capital are reckoned upon an average to amount to one hundred in the month; and for these last three years, one-tenth at least have been emigrants of both sexes!

LETTER XLVI

Paris, *September*, 1805.

My Lord,—Nobody here, except his courtiers, denies that Bonaparte is vain, cruel and ambitious; but as to his private, personal or domestic vices, opinions are various, and even opposite. Most persons, who have long known him, assert that women are his aversion; and many anecdotes have been told of his unnatural and horrid propensities. On the other hand, his seeming attachment to his wife is contradictory to these rumours, which certainly are exaggerated. It is true, indeed, that it was to oblige Barras, and to obtain her fortune, that he accepted of her hand, ten years ago; though insinuating she was far from being handsome, and had long passed the period of inspiring love by her charms. Her husband's conduct towards her may, therefore, be construed perhaps into a proof of indifference towards the whole sex as much as into an evidence of his affection towards her. As he knew *who she was* when he received her from the chaste arms of Barras, and is not unacquainted with her subsequent intrigues—particularly during his stay in Egypt—policy may influence a behaviour which has some resemblance to esteem. He may choose to live with her, but it is impossible he can love her.

A lady, very intimate with Princess Louis Bonaparte, has assured me that, had it not been for Napoleon's *singular* inclination for his youthful step-daughter, he would have divorced his wife the first year of his consulate, and that indirect proposals on that subject had already been made her by Talleyrand. It was then reported that Bonaparte had his eyes fixed upon a Russian princess, and that from the friendship which the late Emperor Paul professed for him, no obstacles to the match were expected to be encountered at St. Petersburg. The untimely end of this prince, and the supplications of his wife and daughter, have since altered his intent, and Madame Napoleon and her children are now, if I may use the expression, incorporated and naturalized with the Bonaparte family.

But what has lately occurred here will better serve to show that Bonaparte is neither averse nor indifferent to the sex. You read last summer in the public prints of the then minister of the interior (Chaptal) being made a senator, and that he was succeeded by our ambassador at Vienna—Champagny. This promotion was the consequence of a disgrace, occasioned by his jealousy of his mistress, a popular actress, Mademoiselle George, one of the handsomest women of this capital. He was informed by his spies that this lady frequently, in the dusk of the evening, or when she thought him employed in his office, went to the house of a famous milliner in the Rue St. Honoré, where, through a door in an adjoining passage, a person, who carefully avoided showing his face, always entered immediately before or after her, and remained as long as she continued there. The house was then by his orders beset with spies, who were to inform him the next time she went to the milliner. To be near at hand, he had hired an apartment in the neighbourhood, where the very next day her visit to the milliner's was announced to him. While his secretary, with four other persons, entered the milliner's house through the street door, Chaptal, with four of his spies, forced the door of the passage open, which was no sooner done than the disguised gallant was found and threatened in the most rude manner by the minister and his companions. He would have been still worse used had not the unexpected appearance of Duroc and a whisper to Chaptal put a stop to the fury of this enraged lover. The *incognito* is said to have been Bonaparte himself, who, the same evening, deprived Chaptal of his ministerial portfolio, and would have sent him to Cayenne, instead of to the senate, had not Duroc dissuaded his Sovereign from giving an *éclat* to an affair which it would be best to bury in oblivion.

Chaptal has never from that day approached Mademoiselle George, and, according to report, Napoleon has also renounced this conquest in favour of Duroc, who is at least her *nominal* gallant. The quantity of jewels with which she has recently been decorated, and displayed with so much ostentation in the new tragedy, *The Templars*, indicate, however, a sovereign rather than a subject for a lover. And, indeed, she already treats the directors of the theatre, her comrades, and even the public, more as a real than a theatrical princess. Without any cause whatever, but from a mere *caprice* to see the camp on the coast, she set out, without leave of absence, and without any previous notice, on the very day she was to play ; and this popular and interesting tragedy was put off for three weeks, until she chose to return to her duty. When complaint was made to the prefects of the palace, now the governors of our theatres, Duroc said that the orders of the Emperor were that no notice should be taken of this *étourderie*, which should not occur again.

Chaptal was, before the Revolution, a bankrupt chemist at Montpellier, having ruined himself in search after the philosopher's stone. To persons in such circumstances, with great presumption, some talents, but no principles, the Revolution could not, with all its anarchy, confusion, and crime, but be a real *blessing*, as Chaptal called it in his *first* speech at the Jacobin Club. Wishing to mimic at Montpellier the taking of the Bastille at Paris, he, in May, 1790, seduced the lower classes and the suburbs to an insurrection, and to an attack on the citadel, which the governor, to avoid all effusion of blood, surrendered without resistance. He was denounced by the municipality to the National Assembly for these and other plots and attempts, but Robespierre and other Jacobins defended him, and he escaped even imprisonment. During 1793 and 1794, he monopolized the contract for making and providing the armies with gunpowder; a favour for which he paid Barrère, Carnot, and other members of the Committee of Public Safety, six millions of livres—£250,000—but by which he pocketed thirty-six millions of livres—£1,500,000—himself. He 'was, under the Directory, menaced with a prosecution for his pillage, but bought it off by a douceur to Rewbel, Barras, and Siéyes. In 1799, he advanced Bonaparte twelve millions of livres—£500,000—to bribe adherents for the new Revolution he meditated, and was in recompense, instead of interest, appointed first counsellor of state; and when Lucien Bonaparte, in September, 1800, was sent on an embassy to Spain, Chaptal succeeded him in the ministry of the interior. You may see by this short account that the chemist Chaptal has, in the Revolution, found the true philosophical stone. He now lives in great style, and has, besides three wives alive (from two of whom he has been divorced), five mistresses, with each a separate establishment. This Chaptal is regarded here as the *most moral* character that has figured in our Revolution, having yet neither committed a single murder nor headed any of our massacres.

LETTER XLVII

PARIS, *September*, 1805.

MY LORD,—I have read a copy of a letter from Madrid, circulated among the members of our foreign diplomatic corps, which draws a most deplorable picture of the Court and Kingdom of Spain. Forced into an unprofitable and expensive war, famine ravaging some, and disease other provinces; experiencing from allies the treatment of tyrannical foes, disunion in his family and among his ministers, His Spanish Majesty totters on a throne exposed to the combined attacks of internal disaffection and external plots, with no other support than the advice of a favourite, who is either a fool or a traitor, and perhaps both.

As the Spanish monarchy has been more humbled and reduced during the twelve years' administration of the Prince of Peace than during the whole period that it has been governed by Princes of the House of Bourbon, the heir of the throne, the young Prince of Asturias, has, with all the moderation consistent with duty, rank and consanguinity, tried to remove an upstart, universally despised for his immorality as well as for his incapacity; and who, should he continue some years longer to rule in the name of Charles IV., will certainly involve his King and his country in one common ruin. Ignorant and presumptuous, even beyond upstarts in general, the Prince of Peace treats with insolence all persons raised above him by birth or talents who refuse to be his accomplices or valets. Proud and certain of the protection of the Queen, and of the weakness of the King, the Spanish nobility is not only humbled, provoked and wronged by him, but openly defied and insulted.

You know the nice principles of honour and loyalty that have always formerly distinguished the ancient families of Spain. Believe me that, notwithstanding what appearances indicate to the contrary, the Spanish grandee who ordered his house to be pulled down because the rebel constable had slept in it, has still many descendants, but loyal men always decline to use that violence to which rebels always resort. Soon after the marriage of the Prince of Asturias, in October, 1801, to his cousin the amiable Marie Antoinette Thérèse, Princess Royal of Naples, the ancient Spanish families sent some deputies to Their Royal Highnesses, not for the purpose of intriguing, but to lay before them the situation of the kingdom, and to inform them of the real cause of all disasters. They were received as faithful subjects and true patriots, and Their Royal

Highnesses promised every support in their power towards remedying the evil complained of, and preventing, if possible, the growth of others.

The Princess of Asturias is a worthy granddaughter of Maria Theresa of Austria, and seems to inherit her character as well as her virtues. She agreed with her royal consort that, after having gained the affection of the Queen by degrees, it would be advisable for her to insinuate some hints of the danger that threatened their country and the discontent that agitated the people. The Prince of Asturias was to act the same part with his father as the Princess did with her mother. As there is no one about the person of Their Spanish Majesties, from the highest lord to the lowest servant, who is not placed there by the favourite and act as his spies, he was soon aware that he had no friend in the heir to the throne. His conversation with Their Majesties confirmed him in this supposition, and that some secret measures were going on to deprive him of the place he occupied, if not of the royal favour. All visitors to the Prince and Princess of Asturias were, therefore, watched by his emissaries; and all the letters or memorials sent to them by the post were opened, read, and, if contrary to his interest, destroyed, and their writers imprisoned in Spain or banished to the colonies. These measures of injustice created suspicion, disunion and perhaps fear, among the members of the Asturian cabal, as it was called: all farther pursuit, therefore, was deferred until more propitious times, and the Prince of Peace remained undisturbed and in perfect security until the rupture with your country last autumn.

It is to be lamented that, with all their valuable qualities and feelings of patriotism, the Prince and Princess of Asturias do not possess a little dissimulation and more knowledge of the world. The favourite tried by all means to gain their good opinion, but his advances met with that repulse they morally deserved, but which, from policy, should have been suspended or softened, with hope of future accommodation.

Beurnonville, the ambassador of our Court to the Court of Madrid, was here upon leave of absence when war was declared by Spain against your country, and his first secretary, Herman, acted as chargé d'affaires. This Herman has been brought up in Talleyrand's office, and is both abler and more artful than Beurnonville; he possesses also the full confidence of our minister, who, in several secret and pecuniary transactions, has obtained many proofs of this secretary's fidelity as well as capacity. The views of the Cabinet of St. Cloud were, therefore, not lost sight of, nor its interest neglected at Madrid.

I suppose you have heard that the Prince of Peace,

like all other ignorant and illiberal people, believes no one can be a good or clever man who is not also his countryman, and that all the ability and probity of the world is confined within the limits of Spain. On this principle he equally detests France and England, Germany and Russia, and is, therefore, not much liked by our Government, except for his imbecility, which makes him its tool and dupe. His disgrace would not be much regretted here, where we have it in our power to place or displace ministers in certain states, whenever and as often as we like. On this occasion, however, we supported him, and helped to dissolve the cabal formed against him: and that for the following reasons.

By the assurances of Beurnonville, Bonaparte and Talleyrand had been led to believe that the Prince and Princess of Asturias were well affected to France, and to them personally; and conceiving themselves much more certain of this than of the good disposition of the favourite, though they did not take a direct part against him, at the same time they did not disclose what they knew was determined on to remove him from the helm of affairs. During Beurnonville's absence, however, Herman had formed an intrigue with a Neapolitan girl, in the suite of the Princess of Asturias, who, influenced by love or bribes, introduced him into the cabinet where her mistress kept her correspondence with her royal parents. With a pick lock key he opened all the drawers, and even the writing-desk, in which he is said to have discovered *written evidence* that, though the Princess was not prejudiced against France, she had but an indifferent opinion of the *morality* and *honesty* of our present Government and of our present governors. One of these original papers Herman appropriated to himself, and despatched to this capital by an extraordinary courier, whose despatches, more than the rupture with your country, forced Beurnonville away in a hurry from the *agreeable* society of gamesters and prostitutes, chiefly frequented by him in this capital.

It is not and cannot be known yet what was the exact plan of the Prince and Princess of Asturias and their adherents; but a diplomatic gentleman, who has just arrived from Madrid, and who can have no reason to impose upon me, has informed me of the following particulars.

Their Royal Highnesses succeeded perfectly in their endeavours to gain the well-merited tenderness and approbation of their Sovereigns in everything else but when the favourite was mentioned with any slight, or when any insinuations were thrown out concerning the mischief arising from his tenacity of power, and incapacity of exercising it with advantage to the State. The Queen was especially irritated when such was the subject of conversation or of remark; and she finally prohibited it under pain of her displeasure. A report even reached Their Royal Highnesses, that the Prince of Peace had demanded their separation and separate confinement. Nothing could, therefore, be effected to impede the progress of wickedness and calamity, but by some temporary measure of severity. In this disagreeable dilemma, it was resolved by the cabal to send the Queen to a convent, until her favourite had been arrested and imprisoned; to declare the Prince of Asturias Regent during the King's illness (His Majesty then still suffered from several paralytic strokes), and to place men of talents and patriotism in the place of the creatures of the Prince of Peace. As soon as this revolution was organized, the Queen would have been restored to full liberty and to that respect due to her rank.

This plan had been communicated to our ambassador, and approved of by our Goverment; but when Herman in such an honest manner had inspected the confidential correspondence of the Princess of Asturias, Beurnonville was instructed by Talleyrand to warn the favourite of the impending danger, and to advise him to be beforehand with his enemies. Instead of telling the truth, the Prince of Peace alarmed the King and Queen with the most absurd fabrications; and assured Their Majesties that their son and their daughter-in-law had determined not only to dethrone them, but to keep them prisoners for life, after they had been forced to witness his execution.

Indolence and weakness are often more fearful than guilt. Everything he said was at once believed : the Prince and Princess were ordered under arrest in their own apartments, without permission to see or correspond with anybody ; and so certain was the Prince of Peace of a complete and satisfactory revenge for the attempt against his tyranny, that a frigate at Cadiz was ready waiting to carry the Princess of Asturias back to Naples. All Spaniards who had the honour of their Sovereigns and of their country at heart lamented these rash proceedings ; but no one dared take any measures to counteract them. At last, however, the Duke of Montemar, grand officer to the Prince of Asturias, demanded an audience of Their Majesties, in the presence of the favourite. He began by begging his Sovereign to recollect that for the place he occupied he was indebted to the Prince of Peace ; and he called upon him to declare whether he had ever had reason to suspect him either of ingratitude or disloyalty. Being answered in the negative, he said that though his present situation and office near the heir to the throne was the pride and desire of his life, he would have thrown it up the instant that he had the least ground to suppose that this Prince ceased to be a dutiful son and subject ; but so far from this being the case, he had observed him in his most unguarded moments—in moments of conviviality had heard him speak of his royal parents with as much submission and respect as if he had been in their presence. "If," continued he, "the Prince of Peace has said otherwise, he has misled his King and his Queen, being, no doubt, deceived himself. To overthrow a throne and to seize it cannot be done without accomplices, without arms, without money. Who are the conspirators hailing the Prince as their chief? I have heard no name but that of the lovely Princess, his consort, the partaker of his sentiments as well as of his heart. And his arms? They are in the hands of those guards his royal parent has given to augment the necessary splendour of his rank. And as to his money? He has none but what is received from royal and paternal munificence and bounty. You, my Prince," said he to the favourite (who seemed much offended at the impression the speech made on Their Majesties), "will one day thank me, if I am happy enough to dissuade dishonourable, impolitic, or unjust sentiments. Of the approbation of posterity I am certain——" "If," interrupted the favourite, "the Prince of Asturias and his consort will give up their bad counsellors, I hope Their Majesties will forget and forgive everything with myself."—"Whether Their Royal Highnesses," replied the Duke of Montemar, "have done anything that deserves

forgiveness, or whether they have any counsellors, I do not
know, and am incompetent to judge: but I am much
mistaken in the character of Their Royal Highnesses if they
wish to purchase favour at the expense of confidence and
honour. An order from His Majesty may immediately clear
up this doubt." The Prince of Peace was then ordered to
write, in the name of the King, to his children in the
manner he proposed, and to command an answer by the
messenger. In half-an-hour the messenger returned with a
letter addressed to the favourite, containing only these lines:
"A King of Spain is well aware that a Prince and Princess
of Asturias can have no answer to give to such proposals
or to such questions." After six days' arrest, and after the
Prince of Peace had in vain endeavoured to discover something
to inculpate Their Royal Highnesses, they were invited
to Court, and reconciled both to him and their royal parents.

LETTER XLVIII

Paris, *September*, 1805.

My Lord,—I will add in this letter, to the communication of the gentlemen mentioned in my last, what I remember myself of the letter which was circulated among our diplomatists, concerning the intrigues at Madrid.

The Prince of Peace, before he listened to the advice of Duke de Montemar, had consulted Beurnonville, who dissuaded all violence, and as much as possible all noise. This accounts for the favourite's pretended moderation on this occasion. But though he was externally reconciled, and, as was reported at Madrid, *had sworn his reconciliation even by taking the sacrament,* all the undertakings of the Prince and Princess of Asturias were strictly observed and reported by the spies whom he had placed round Their Royal Highnesses. Vain of his success and victory, he even lost that respectful demeanour which a good, nay, a well-bred subject always shows to the heir to the throne, and the Princes related to his Sovereign. He sometimes behaved with a premeditated familiarity, and with an insolence provoking or defying resentment. It was on the days of great festivities, when the Court was most brilliant, and the courtiers most numerous, that he took occasion to be most arrogant to those whom he traitorously and audaciously dared to call his rivals. On the 9th of last December, at the celebration of the Queen's birthday, his conduct towards Their Royal Highnesses excited such general indignation that the remembrance of the occasion of the fête, and the presence of their Sovereigns, could not repress a murmur, which made the favourite tremble. A signal from the Prince of Asturias would then have been sufficient to have caused the insolent upstart to be seized and thrown out of the window. I am told that some of the Spanish grandees even laid their hands on their swords, fixing their eyes on the heir to the throne, as if to say: "Command, and your unworthy enemy shall exist no more."

To prepare, perhaps, the royal and paternal mind for deeds which contemporaries always condemn, and posterity will always reprobate, the Prince of Peace procured a history to be written *in his own way and manner*, of Don Carlos, the unfortunate son of the barbarous and unnatural Philip II.; but the Queen's confessor, though, like all her other domestics, a tool of the favourite, threw it into the fire with reproof, saying that Spain did not remember in Philip II. the grand and powerful monarch, but abhorred in him the royal assassin; adding that no laws, human or divine, no institutions, no supremacy whatever, could authorize a parent to stain his hands in the blood of his children.—These anecdotes are sufficient both to elucidate the inveteracy of the favourite, the abject state of the heir to the throne, and the incomprehensible infatuation of the King and Queen.

Our ambassador in the meantime dissembled always with the Prince and Princess of Asturias; and even made them understand that he disapproved of those occurrences so disagreeable to them; but he neither offered to put an end to them, nor to be a mediator for a perfect reconciliation with their Sovereigns. He was guided by no other motive but to keep the favourite in subjection and alarm by preserving a correspondence with his rivals. That this was the case and the motive cannot be doubted from the financial intrigue he carried on in the beginning of last month.

Foreigners have but an imperfect or erroneous idea of the amount of the immense sums Spain has paid to our Government in loans, in contributions, in donations and in subsidies. Since the reign of Bonaparte, or for these last five years, upwards of half the revenue of the Spanish monarchy has either been brought into our national treasury or into the privy purse of the Bonaparte family. Without the aid of Spanish money, neither would our gunboats have been built, our fleets equipped, nor our armies paid. The dreadful situation of the Spanish finances is, therefore, not surprising—it is, indeed, still more surprising that a general bankruptcy has not already involved the Spanish nation in a general ruin.

When, on his return from Italy, the recall of the Russian negotiator and the preparations of Austria convinced Bonaparte of the probability of a Continental war, our troops on the coast had not been paid for two months, and his imperial ministers of finances had no funds either to discharge the arrears or to provide for future payments until the beginning of the year 14, or the 22nd instant. Beurnonville was, therefore, ordered to demand peremptorily from the Cabinet of Madrid forty millions of livres—£1,666,000 *in advance* upon future subsidies. Half of that sum had, indeed, shortly before arrived at Cadiz from America, but much more was due by the Spanish Government to its own creditors, and promised them in payment of old debts. The Prince of Peace, in consequence, declared that, however much he wished to oblige the French Government, it was utterly impossible to procure, much less to advance such sums. Beurnonville then became more assiduous than ever about the Prince and Princess of Asturias; and he had the impudence to assert that they had promised, if their friends were at the head of affairs, to satisfy the wishes and expectation of the Emperor of the French, by seizing the treasury at

Cadiz, and paying the State creditors in *vales deinero*: notes hitherto payable in cash, and never at a discount. The stupid favourite swallowed the palpable bait: four millions in dollars were sent under an escort to this country, while the Spanish notes instantly fell to a discount at first of four and afterwards of six per cent., and probably will fall lower still, as no treasures are expected from America this autumn. It was with two millions of these dollars that the credit of the Bank of France was restored, or at least *for some time* enabled to resume its payments in specie. Thus wretched Spain pays abroad for the forging of those disgraceful fetters which oppress her at home: and supports a foreign tyranny, which finally must produce domestic misery as well as slavery.

When the Prince and Princess of Asturias were informed of the scandalous and false assertion of Beurnonville, they and their adherents not only publicly, and in all societies, contradicted it, but affirmed that, rather than obtain authority or influence on such ruinous terms, they would have consented to remain discarded and neglected during their lives. They took the more care to have their sentiments known on this subject, as our ambassador's calumny had hurt their popularity. It was then first that, to revenge the shame with which his duplicity had covered him, Beurnonville permitted and persuaded the Prince of Peace *to begin* the chastisement of Their Royal Highnesses in the persons of their favourites. Duke de Montemar, the grand officer to the Prince of Asturias ; Marquis de Villa Franca, the grand equerry to the Princess of Asturias ; Count de Miranda, chamberlain to the King ; and the Countess Dowager del Monte, with six other Court ladies and four other noblemen, were, therefore, exiled from Madrid into different provinces, and forbidden to reside in any *place* within twenty leagues of the residence of the royal family. According to the last letters and communications from Spain, the Prince and Princess of Asturias had not appeared at Court since the insult offered them in the disgrace of their friends, and were resolved not to appear in any place where they might be likely to meet with the favourite.

Among our best informed politicians here, it is expected that a revolution and a change of dynasty will be the issue of this our political embryo in Spain. Napoleon has more than once indirectly hinted that the Bonaparte dynasty will never be firm and fixed in France as long as any Bourbons reign in Spain or Italy. Should he prove victorious in the present Continental contest, another peace, and not the most advantageous, will again be signed with your country

a peace which, I fear, will leave him absolute master of all Continental states. His family arrangements are publicly avowed to be as follow : His third brother, Louis, and his sons, are to be the heirs of the French Empire. Joseph Bonaparte is, at the death or resignation of Napoleon, to succeed to the kingdom of Italy, including Naples. Lucien, though at present in disgrace, is considered as the person destined to supplant the Bourbons in Spain, where, during his embassy in 1800, and in 1801, he formed certain *connections* which Napoleon still keeps up and preserves. Holland will be the inheritance of Jerome should Napoleon not live long enough to extend his power in Great Britain. Such are the *modest* pretensions our imperial courtiers bestow upon the family of our Sovereign.

As to the Prince of Peace, he is only an imbecile instrument in the hands of our intriguers and innovators, which they make use of as long as they find it necessary, and which, when that ceases to be the case, they break and throw away. This idiot is made to believe that both his political and physical existence depends entirely upon our support, and he has infused the same ridiculous notion into his accomplices and adherents. Guilt, ignorance and cowardice thus misled may, directed by art, interest and craft, perform wonders to entangle themselves in the destruction of their country.

Beurnonville, our present ambassador at Madrid, is the son of a porter, and was a porter himself when, in 1770, he enlisted as a soldier in one of our regiments serving in the

East Indies. Having there collected some pillage, he purchased the place of a major in the militia of the Island of Bourbon, but was for his immorality broken by the governor. Returning to France, he bitterly complained of this *injustice*, and, after much cringing in the ante-chambers of ministers, he obtained at last the Cross of St. Louis as a kind of indemnity. About the same time he also bought with his Indian wealth the place of an officer in the Swiss Guard of Monsieur, the present Louis XVIII. Being refused admittance into any genteel societies, he resorted with Barras and other disgraced nobles to gambling-houses, and he even kept two himself when the Revolution took place. He had at the same time, and for a *certain* interest, advanced Madame d'Estainville money to establish her famous, or rather infamous, house in the Rue de Bonnes Enfants, near the Palais Royal—a house that soon became the fashionable resort of our friends of Liberty and Equality.

In 1790, Beurnonville offered his services as aide-de-camp to our then hero of great ambition and small capacity, La Fayette, who declined the *honour*. The Jacobins were not so nice. In 1792, they appointed him a general under Dumouriez, who baptised him his Ajax. This modern Ajax, having obtained a separate command, attacked Trèves in a most ignorant manner, and was worsted with great loss. The official reports of our revolutionary generals have long been admired for their *modesty* as well as *veracity;* but Beurnonville has almost outdone them all, not excepting our great Bonaparte. In a report to the National Convention concerning a terrible engagement of three hours near Grewenmacker, Beurnonville declares that, though the number of the enemy killed was immense, his troops got out of the scrape with the loss of only *the little finger of one of his riflemen.* On the 4th of February, 1793, a fortnight after the execution of Louis XVI., he was nominated minister of the War Department—a place which he refused under a pretence that he was better able to serve his country with his sword than with his pen, having already been *in one hundred and twenty battles* (where, he did not enumerate or state). On the 14th of the following March, however, he accepted the ministerial portfolio, which he did not keep long, being delivered up by his Hector, Dumouriez, to the Austrians. He remained a prisoner at Olmutz until the 22nd of November, 1795, when he was included among the persons exchanged for the daughter of Louis XVI., her present Royal Highness the Duchess of Angoulême.

In the autumn of 1796 he had a temporary command of the dispersed remnants of Jourdan's army, and in 1797 he was sent as a French commander to Holland. In 1799, Bonaparte appointed him an ambassador to the Court of Berlin; and in 1803 removed him in the same character to the Court of Madrid. In Prussia, his *talents* did not cause him to be dreaded, nor did his personal qualities make him esteemed. In France he is laughed at as a boaster, but not trusted as a warrior. In Spain he is neither dreaded nor esteemed, neither laughed at nor courted; he is there universally despised. He studies to be thought a gentleman; but the native porter breaks through the veil of a ridiculously affected and *outré* politeness. Notwithstanding the complacent grimaces of his face, the self-sufficiency of his looks, his systematically powdered and dressed hair, his showy dress, his counted and short bows, and his presumptuous conversation, teeming with ignorance, vulgarity and obscenity, he cannot escape even the most inattentive observer.

The ambassador, Beurnonville, is now between fifty and sixty years of age; is a grand officer of our Imperial Legion of Honour; has a brother who is a turnkey, and two sisters, one married to a tailor, and another to a merchant who cries dogs' and cats' meat in our streets.

LETTER XLIX

PARIS, *September*, 1805.

MY LORD,— Bonaparte did not at first intend to take his wife with him when he set out for Strasburg; but her tears, the effect of her *tenderness* and *apprehension* for his person, at last altered his resolution. Madame Napoleon, to tell the truth, does not like much to be in the power of Joseph, nor even in that of her son-in-law, Louis Bonaparte, should any accident make her a widow.

During the Emperor's absence the former is the president of the senate, and the latter the governor of this capital and commander of the troops in the interior; so that the one dictates the Senatus Consultum, in case of a vacancy of the throne, and the other supports these civil determinations with his military forces. Even with the army in Germany, Napoleon's brother-in-law, Murat, is as a pillar of the Bonaparte dynasty, and to prevent the intrigues and plots of other generals from an imperial diadem; while, in Italy, his step-son, Eugenius de Beauharnais, as a viceroy, commands even the commander-in-chief, Massena. It must be granted that the Emperor has so ably taken his precautions that it is almost certain that, *at first*, his orders will be obeyed, even after his death; and the will deposited by him in the senate, without opposition, carried into execution. These very precautions evince, however, how uncertain and precarious he looks upon his existence to be, and that, notwithstanding addresses and oaths, he apprehends that the Bonaparte dynasty will not survive him.

Most of the generals now employed by him are either of his own creation, or men on whom he has conferred rank and wealth, which they might consider unsafe under any other prince but a Bonaparte. The superior officers, not included in the above description, are such insignificant characters that, though he makes use of their experience and courage, he does not fear their views or ambition. Among the inferior officers, and even among the men, all those who have displayed, either at reviews or in battles, capacity, activity or valour, are all members of his Legion of Honour; and are bound to him by the double tie of gratitude and self-interest. They look to him alone for future advancements, and for the preservation of the distinction they have obtained from him. His emissaries artfully disseminate that a Bourbon would inevitably overthrow everything a Bonaparte has erected; and that all military and civil officers rewarded or favoured by Napoleon the First will not only be discarded, but disgraced, and perhaps punished, by a Louis XVIII. Any person who would be imprudent enough to attempt to prove the impossibility, as well as the absurdity, of these impolitic and retrospective measures, would be instantly taken up and shot as an emissary of the Bourbons.

I have often amused myself in conversing with our new generals and new officers; there is such a curious mixture of ignorance and information, of credulity and disbelief, of real boasting and affected modesty, in everything they say or do in company; their manners are far from being elegant, but also very distant from vulgarity; they do not resemble those of what we formerly called *gens comme il faut*, and *la bonne société;* nor those of the bourgeoisie, or the lower classes. They form a new species of fashionables, and a *haut ton militaire*, which strikes a person accustomed to Courts at first with surprise, and perhaps with indignation: though, after a time, those of our sex at least become reconciled, if not pleased with it, because there is a kind of military frankness interwoven with the military roughness. Our ladies, however (I mean those who have seen other Courts, or remember our other coteries), complain loudly of this alteration of address, and of this fashionable innovation: and pretend that our military, under the notion of being frank, are rude, and by the negligence of their manners and language, are not only offensive, but inattentive and indelicate. This is so much the more provoking to them, as our imperial courtiers and imperial placemen do not think themselves fashionable without imitating our military gentry, who take Napoleon for their exclusive model and chief in everything, even in manners.

What I have said above only applies to those officers whose parents are not of the lowest class, or who entered so early or so young into the army that they may be said to have been educated there, and as they advanced, have assumed the *ton* of their comrades of the same rank. I was invited, some time ago, to a wedding, by a jeweller whose sister had been my nurse, and whose daughter was to be married to a captain of hussars quartered here. The bridegroom had engaged several other officers to assist at the ceremony, and to partake of the fête and ball that followed. A general of the name of Liebeau was also of the party, and obtained the place of honour by the side of the bride's mother. At his entrance into the apartment I formed an opinion of him which his subsequent conduct during the ball confirmed.

During the dinner he seemed to forget that he had a knife and a fork, and he did not eat of a dish (and he ate of them all, numerous as they were) without bespattering or besmearing himself or his neighbours. He broke two glasses and one plate, and, for equality's sake, I suppose, when he threw the wine on the lady to his right, the lady to his left was inundated with sauces. In getting up from dinner to take coffee and liqueurs, according to our custom, as he took the hand of the mistress of the house, he seized at the same time a corner of the napkin, and was not aware of his blunder till the destruction of bottles, glasses and plates, and the screams of the ladies, informed him of the havoc and terror his awkward gallantry had occasioned. When the ball began, he was too vain of his rank and precedency to suffer anyone else to lead the bride down the first dance; but she was not, I believe, much obliged to him for his politeness; it cost her the tail of her wedding-gown and a broken nail, and she continued lame during the remainder of the night. In making an apology to her for his want of dexterity, and assuring her that he was not so awkward in handling the enemies of his country in battle as in handing the friends he esteemed in a dance, he gave no quarter to an old maiden aunt, whom, in the violence of his gesticulation, he knocked down with his elbow and laid sprawling on the ground. He was sober when these accidents literally occurred.

Of this original I collected the following particulars:

Before the Revolution he was a soldier in the regiment of Flanders, from which he deserted and became a corporal in another regiment; in 1793 he was a drum-major in one of the battalions in garrison in Paris. You remember the struggles of factions in the latter part of May and in the beginning of June, the same year, when Brissot and his accomplices were contending with Marat, Robespierre and their adherents for the reins of power. On the 1st of June the latter party could not get a drummer to beat the alarm, though they offered money and advancement. At last Robespierre stepped forward to Liebeau and said, "Citizen, beat the alarm march, and to-day you shall be nominated a general." Liebeau obeyed, Robespierre became victorious and kept his promise, and thus my present associate gained his rank. He has since been employed under Jourdan in Germany, and under Le Courbe in Switzerland. When, under the former, he was ordered to retreat towards the Rhine, he pointed out the march route to his division according to his geographical knowledge, but mistook upon the map the River Main for a turnpike road, and commanded the retreat accordingly. Ever since, our troops have called that river *La chausée de Liebeau*. He was not more fortunate in Helvetia. Being ordered to cross one of the mountains, he marched his men into a *glacier*, where twelve perished before he was aware of his mistake.

Being afterwards appointed a governor of Blois, he there became a petty, insupportable tyrant, and laid all the inhabitants indiscriminately under arbitrary contribution. Those who refused to pay were imprisoned as aristocrats, and their property confiscated in the name and on the part of the nation; that is to say, he appropriated to himself in the name of the nation everything that struck his fancy: and if any complaints were made, the owners were seized and sent to the Revolutionary Tribunal at Paris to be condemned as the correspondents or adherents of the royalists of La Vendée. After the death of Robespierre, he was deprived of this profitable place, in which, during the short space of eleven months, he amassed five millions of livres—£208,000. The Directory then gave him a division, first under Jourdan, and afterwards under Le Courbe. Bonaparte, after witnessing his incapacity in Italy, in 1800, put him on the *full* half-pay, and has lately made him a commander of the Legion of Honour.

His dear spouse, Madame Liebeau, is his counterpart. When he married her, she was crying mackerel and herrings in our streets: but she told me in confidence, during the dinner, being seated by my side, that her father was an officer of fortune, and a Chevalier of the Order of St. Louis. She assured me that her husband had done greater services to his country than Bonaparte: and that, had it not been for his patriotism in 1793, the Austrians would have taken Paris. She was very angry with Madame Napoleon, to whom she had been presented, but who had not shown her so much attention and civility as was due to her husband's rank, having never invited her to more than one supper and two tea-parties: and when invited by her, had sent Duroc with an apology that she was unable to come, though the same evening she went to the opera.

Another guest, in the regimentals of a colonel, seemed rather bashful when I spoke to him. I could not comprehend the reason, and therefore enquired of our host who he was. (You know that with us it is not the custom to introduce persons by name, &c., as in your country, when meeting in mixed companies.) He answered, "Do you not remember your brother's jockey, Frial?"
"Yes," said I, "but he was established by my brother as a hairdresser."—"He is the very same person," replied the jeweller. "He has fought very bravely, and is now a colonel of dragoons, a great favourite with Bonaparte, and will be a general at the first promotion." As the colonel did not seem to desire a renewal of acquaintance with me, I did not intrude myself upon him.

During the supper the military gentlemen were encouraged by the bridegroom, and the bottle went round very freely; and the more they drank, the greater and more violent became their political discussions. Liebeau vociferated in favour of republican and revolutionary measures, and avowed his approbation of requisitions, confiscations, and the guillotine : while Frial inclined to the regular and organized despotism of one, to secret trial, and still more secret executions ; defending arbitrary imprisonments, exiles and transportations. This displeased Madame Liebeau, who exclaimed, " Since the colonel is so fond of an imperial government, he can have no objection to remain a faithful subject whenever my husband, Liebeau, becomes an Antoine the First, Emperor of the French." Frial smiled with contempt. "You seem to think it improbable," said Libeau. " I, Antoine Liebeau—I have more prospect of being an Emperor than Napoleon Bonaparte had ten years ago, when he was only a colonel, and arrested as a terrorist. And am I not a Frenchman ? And is he not a foreigner ? Come, shake hands with me ; as soon as I am an Emperor, depend upon it you shall be a general, and a grand officer of the Legion of Honour."—"Ah ! my jewel," interrupted Madame Liebeau, " how happy will France then be. You are such a friend of peace. We will then have no wars, no contributions ; all the English milords may then come here and spend their money, nobody cares about where or how. Will you not, then, my sweet love, make all the gentlemen here your chamberlains, and permit me to accept of all the ladies of the company for my maids-of-honour or ladies-in-waiting?"

"Softly, softly," cried Frial, who now began to be as intoxicated and as ambitious as the general: "whenever Napoleon dies, I have more hope, more claim, and more right than you to the throne. I am in actual service; and had not Bonaparte been the same, he might have still remained upon the half-pay, obscure and despised. Were not most of the field-marshals and generals under him now, above him ten years ago? May I not, ten years hence, if I am satisfied with you, General Liebeau, make you also a field-marshal, or my minister of war; and you, Madame Liebeau, a lady of my wife's wardrobe, as soon as I am married? I, too, have my plans and my views, and perhaps one day you will recollect this conversation, and not be sorry for my acquaintance." "What! you a colonel, an Emperor, before me, who have so long been a general?" howled Liebeau, who was no longer able to speak. "I would sooner knock your brains out with this bottle than suffer such a precedence; and my wife a lady of your wardrobe! she who has possessed from her birth the soul of an Empress! No, sir! never will I take the oath to you, nor suffer anybody else to take it."—"Then I will punish you as a rebel," retorted Frial: "and as sure as you stand here you shall be shot."

Liebeau then rose up to' fetch his sword, but the company interfered, and the dispute about the priority of claim to the throne of France between the *ci-devant* drummer and *ci-devant* jockey was left undecided. From the words and looks of several of the captains present, I think that they seemed, in their own opinions, to have as much prospect and expectation to reign over the French empire as either General Liebeau or Colonel Frial.

As soon as I returned home I wrote down this curious conversation and this debate about supremacy. To what a degradation is the highest rank in my unfortunate country reduced when two such personages seriously contend about it! I collected more subjects for meditation and melancholy in this low company (where, by-the-bye, I witnessed more vulgarity and more indecencies than I had before seen during my life) than from all former scenes of humiliation and disgust since my return here. When I the next day mentioned it to General de M——, whom you have known as an emigrant officer in your service, but whom policy has since ranged under the colours of Bonaparte, he assured me that these discussions about the imperial throne are very frequent among the superior officers, and have caused many bloody scenes; and that hardly any of our generals of any talent exist who have not the same *arrière pensée* of some day or other. Napoleon cannot, therefore, well be ignorant of the many other dynasties here now rivalling that of the Bonapartes, and who wait only for his exit to tear his Senatus Consultum, his will, and his family, as well as each other, to pieces.

LETTER L.

Paris, *September*, 1805.

My Lord,—I was lately invited to a tea-party by one of our rich upstarts, who, from a scavenger, is, by the Revolution and by Bonaparte, transformed into a legislator, commander of the Legion of Honour, and possessor of wealth amounting to eighteen millions of livres—£750,000. In this house I saw for the first time the famous Madame Chevalier, the mistress, and the indirect cause of the untimely end, of the unfortunate Paul the First. She is very short, fat and coarse. I do not know whether prejudice, from what I have heard of her vile, greedy and immoral character, influenced my feelings, but she appeared to me a most artful, vain and disagreeable woman. She looked to be about thirty-six years of age; and though she might when younger have been well made, it is impossible that she could ever have been handsome. The features of her face are far from being regular. Her mouth is large, her eyes hollow, and her nose short. Her language is that of brothels, and her manners correspond with her expressions. She is the daughter of a workman at a silk manufactory at

Lyons; she ceased to be a maid before she had attained the age of a woman, and lived in a brothel in her native city, kept by a Madame Thibault, where her husband first became acquainted with her. Having then a tolerably good voice, and being young and insinuating, he introduced her on the same stage where he was one of the inferior dancers. Here in a short time she improved so much, that she was engaged as a supernumerary; her salary in France as an actress was, however, never above twelve hundred livres in the year—£50—which was four hundred livres more than her husband received.

He, with several other inferior and unprincipled actors and dancers, quitted the stage in the beginning of the Revolution for the clubs; and instead of diverting his audience, resolved to reform and regenerate his nation. His name is found in the annals of the crimes perpetrated at Lyons, by the side of that of a Fouché, a Collot d'Herbois, and other wicked offsprings of rebellion. With all other terrorists, he was imprisoned for some time after the death of Robespierre: as soon as restored to liberty, he set out with his wife for Hamburg, where some amateurs had constructed a French theatre.

It was in the autumn of 1795 when Madame Chevalier was first heard of in the North of Europe, where her arrival occasioned a kind of theatrical war between the French,

American and Hamburg Jacobins on one side, and the English and emigrant loyalists on the other. Having no money to continue her pretended journey to Sweden, she asked the manager of the French theatre at Hamburg to allow her a benefit, and to play on that night. She selected, of course, a part in which she could appear to the most advantage, and was deservedly applauded. The very next evening the Jacobin cabal called the manager upon the stage, and insisted that Madame Chevalier should be given a regular engagement. He replied that no place suitable to her talents was vacant, and that it would be ungenerous to turn away for her sake another actress with whom the public had hitherto declared their satisfaction. The Jacobins continued inflexible, and here, as well as everywhere else, supported injustice by violence. As the *patriotism* of the husband, more than the charms of the wife, was known to have produced this indecent fracas, which for upwards of a week interrupted the plays, all anti-Jacobins united to restore order. In this they would, perhaps, have finally succeeded, had not the bayonets of the Hamburg soldiers interfered, and forced this precious piece of revolutionary furniture upon the manager and upon the stage.

After displaying her gratitude *in her own way* to each individual of the Jacobin levy *en masse* in her favour, she was taken into keeping by a then rich and married Hamburg merchant, who made her a present of a richly and elegantly furnished house, and expended besides ten thousand louis d'or on her, before he had a mortifying conviction that some other had partaken of those favours for which he had so dearly paid. A countryman of yours then showed himself with more noise than honour upon the scene, and made his *début* with a phaeton and four, which he presented to his theatrical goddess, together with his own dear portrait, set round with large and valuable diamonds. Madame Chevalier, however, soon afterwards hearing that her English gallant had come over to Germany for economy, and that his credit with his banker was nearly exhausted, had his portrait changed for that of another and richer lover, preserving, however, the diamonds; and she exposed this inconstancy even upon the stage, by suspending, as if in triumph, the new portrait fastened on her bosom. The Englishman, wishing to retrieve his phaeton and horses, which he protested only to have lent his belle, found that she had put the whole equipage into a kind of lottery, or raffle, to which all her numerous *friends* had subscribed, and that an Altona Jew had won it.

- The successor of your countryman was a Russian nobleman, succeeded in his turn by a Polish Jew, who was ruined and discarded within three months. She then became the property of the public, and, by her active *industry*, during a stay of four years at Hamburg, she was enabled to remit to France, before her departure for Russia, one million two hundred thousand livres—£50,000. Her popularity was, however, at that period, very much on the decline, as she had stooped to the most indelicate means to collect money, and to extort it from her friends and acquaintances. She had always lists of subscriptions in her pocket; some, with proposals to play in her lotteries for trinkets unnecessary to her; others, to procure her, by the assistance of subscribers, some trinkets which she wanted.

I suppose it to be no secret to you that the female agents of Talleyrand's *secret* diplomacy are frequently more useful than those of the other sex. I am told that Madame Rochechouart was that *friend* of our minister who engaged Madame Chevalier in her Russian expedition, and who instructed her how to act her parts well at St. Petersburg. I need not repeat what is so well known, that, after this artful emissary had ruined the domestic happiness of the Russian monarch, she degraded him in his political transactions, and became the indirect cause of his untimely end, in procuring, for a bribe of fifty thousand roubles in money and jewels, the recall of P—— Z——, one of the principal conspirators against the unfortunate Paul.

The wealth she plundered in the Russian capital

within the short period of twenty months, amounted to much above one million of roubles. For money she procured impunity for crime, and brought upon innocence the punishment merited by guilt. The scaffolds of Russia were bleeding, and the roads to Siberia crowded with the victims of the avarice of this female demon, who often promised what she was unable to perform, and, to silence complaint, added cruelty to fraud, and, after pocketing the bribe, resorted to the executioner to remove those whom she had duped. The shocking anecdote of the Sardinian secretary, whom she swindled out of nearly a hundred thousand roubles, and on whom she afterwards persuaded her imperial lover to inflict capital punishment, is too recent and too public to be unknown or forgotten. A Russian nobleman has assured me that the number of unfortunate individuals whom her and her husband's intrigues have caused to suffer capitally during 1800 and 1801 was forty-six; and that nearly three hundred persons besides, who could not or would not pay their extortionate demands, were exiled to Siberia during the same period of time.

You may, perhaps, think that a low woman who could produce such great and terrible events, must be mistress of natural charms as well as of acquired accomplishments. As I have already stated, she can have no pretensions to either, but she is extremely insinuating, sings tolerably well, has a fresh and healthy look, and possesses an unusually good share of cunning, presumption and duplicity. Her husband, also, everywhere took care to make her fashionable; and the vanity of the first of their dupes increased the number of her admirers and engaged the vanity of others in their turn to sacrifice themselves at her shrine.

The immorality of our age, also, often procured her popularity for what deserved, and in better times would have encountered, the severest reprobation. In 1797, an emigrant lodged at an inn at Hamburg where another traveller was robbed of a large sum in ready money and jewels. The unfortunate is always suspected: and in the visit made to his room by the magistrates was found a key that opened the door of the apartment where the theft had been committed. In vain did he represent that, had he been the thief he should not have kept an instrument which was, or might be, construed into an argument of guilt; he was carried to prison, and, though none of the property was discovered in his possession, would have been condemned had he not produced Madame Chevalier, who avowed that the key opened the door of her bedroom, which the smith who had made it confirmed, and swore that he had fabricated eight other keys for the same actress, and for the same purpose.

At that time this woman lived in the same house with

her husband, but cohabited there with the husband of another woman. She had also places of assignation with other gallants at private apartments, both in Hamburg and at Altona. All these her scandalous intrigues were known even to the common porters of these cities. The first time, after the affair of the key had become public, she acted in a play where a key was mentioned, and the audience immediately repeated, "The key! the key!" Far from being ashamed, she appeared every night in pieces selected by her where there was mention of keys, and thus tired the jokes of the public. This impudence might have been expected from her, but it was little to be supposed that her barefaced vices should, as really was the case, augment the crowd of suitors, and occasion even some duels, which latter she both encouraged and rewarded.

Two brothers, of the name of de S——, were both in love with her, and the eldest, as the richest, became her choice. Offended at his refusal of too large a sum of money, she wrote to the younger de S——, and offered to accede to his proposals if, like a gentleman, he would avenge the affront she had experienced from his brother. He consulted a friend, who, to expose her infamy, advised him to send some confidential person to inform her that he had killed his elder brother and expected the recompense on the same night. He went and was received with open arms, and had just retired with her, when the elder brother, accompanied by his friend, entered the room. Madame Chevalier, instead of upbraiding, laughed, and the next day the public laughed with her and applauded her more than ever. She knew very well what she was doing. The stories of the key and the duel produced for her more than four thousand louis d'or by the number of new gallants they enticed. It was a kind of emulation among all young men in the North who should be foremost to dishonour and ruin himself with this infamous woman.

Madame Chevalier and her husband now live here in grand style, and have their grand parties, grand teas, grand assemblies and grand balls. Their hotel, I am assured, is even visited by the Bonapartes and by the members of the foreign diplomatic corps. In the house where I saw her, I observed that Louis Bonaparte and two foreign ambassadors spoke to her as old acquaintances. Though rich, to the amount of ten millions of livres—£416,000—she, or rather her husband, keeps a gambling-house, and her superannuated charms are still to be bought for money, at the disposal of those amateurs who are fond of antiques. Both her husband and herself are still members of our secret diplomacy, though she complains loudly that of the two millions of livres £83,000 promised her in 1799 by Bonaparte and Talleyrand, if she could succeed in persuading Paul I. to withdraw from his alliance with England and Austria, only six hundred thousand livres—£25,000 has been paid her.

I cannot finish this letter without telling you that before our military forces had reached the Rhine, our political incendiaries had already taken the field, and were in full march towards the Austrian, Russian and Prussian capitals. The advanced guard of this dangerous corps consists entirely of females, all gifted with beauty and parts as much superior to those of Madame Chevalier as their instructions are better digested. Bonaparte and Talleyrand have more than once regretted that Madame Chevalier was not ordered to enter into the conspiracy against Paul (whose inconsistency and violence they foresaw would make his reign short), that she might have influenced the conspirators to fix upon a successor more pliable and less scrupulous, and who would have suffered the Cabinet of St. Cloud to dictate to the Cabinet of St. Petersburg.

I dined in company several times this last spring with two ladies who, rumour said, have been destined for your P—— of W—— and D—— of Y—— ever since the Peace of Amiens. Talleyrand is well informed what figures and what talents are requisite to make an impression on these princes, and has made his choice accordingly. These ladies have lately disappeared, and when inquired after are stated to be in the country, though I do not consider it improbable that they have already arrived at headquarters. They are both rather fair and lusty, above the middle size, and about twenty-five years of age. They speak, besides French, the English and Italian languages. They are good drawers, good musicians, good singers, and, if necessary, even good drinkers.

LETTER LI

PARIS, *September*, 1805.

MY LORD,—Had the citizens of the United States been as submissive to the taxation of your Government as to the vexations of our ruler, America would, perhaps, have been less free and Europe more tranquil.

After the Treaty of Amiens had produced a general pacification, our Government was seriously determined to reconquer from America a part of those treasures its citizens had gained during the revolutionary war, by a neutrality which our policy and interest required, and which the liberality of your Government endured. Hence the acquisition we made of New Orleans from Spain, and hence the intrigues of our emissaries in that colony, and the peremptory requisitions of provision for St. Domingo by our minister and our generals. Had we been victorious in St. Domingo, most of our troops there were destined for the American Continent, to invade, according to circumstances, either the Spanish colonies on the *terra firma* or the States of the American Commonwealth. The unforeseen rupture with your country postponed a plan that is far from being laid aside.

You may, perhaps, think that since we sold Louisiana we have no footing in America that can threaten the peace or independence of the United States; but may not the same dictates that procured us at Madrid the acquisition of New Orleans, also make us masters of Spanish Florida? And do you believe it improbable that the present disagreement between America and Spain is kept up by our intrigues and by our future views? Would not a word from us settle in an instant at Madrid the differences as well as the frontiers of the contending parties in America? And does it not seem to be the regular and systematic plan of our Government to provoke the retaliation of the Americans, and to show our disregard of their privilege of neutrality and rights of independence; and that we insult them only because we despise them, and despise them only because we do not apprehend their resentment?

I have heard the late American minister here assert that the American vessels captured by our cruisers and condemned by our tribunals, only during the last war, amounted to above five hundred; and their cargoes (all American property) to one hundred and fifty millions of livres £6,000,000. Some few days ago I saw a printed list, presented by the American consul to our minister of the marine department, claiming one hundred and twelve American ships captured in the West Indies and on the coast of America within these last two years, the cargoes of which have all been confiscated, and most of the crews still continue prisoners at Martinico, at Guadeloupe or Cayenne. Besides these, sixty-six American ships, after being plundered in part of their cargoes at sea by our privateers, had been released ; and their claims for property thus lost, or damage thus done, amounted to one million three hundred thousand livres £54,000.

You must have read the proclamations of our governors in the West Indies, and therefore remember that one dated at Guadeloupe, and another dated at the City of San Domingo, both declare, without farther ceremony, all American and other neutral ships and cargoes good and lawful prizes, when coming from or destined to any port in the Island of St. Domingo, because *Bonaparte's subjects there were in a state of rebellion.* What would these philanthropists who, twelve years ago, wrote so many libels against your ministers for their pretended system of famine, have said, had they, instead of prohibiting the carrying of ammunition and provisions to the ports of France, thus extended their orders without discrimination or distinction? How would the neutral Americans, and the neutral Danes, and their then allies, *philosophers* and Jacobins of all colours and classes, have complained and declaimed against the tyrants of the seas; against the enemies of humanity, liberty and equality. Have not the negroes now, as much as our Jacobins had in 1793, a right to call upon all those tender-hearted schemers, dupes or impostors, to interest humanity in their favour? But as far as I know, no friends of liberty have yet written a line in favour of these oppressed and injured men, whose former slavery was never doubtful, and who, therefore, had more reason to rise against their tyrants, and to attempt to shake off their yoke, than our French insurgents, who, free before, have never since they revolted against lawful authority enjoyed an hour's freedom. But the Emperor Jacques the First has no propagators, no emissaries, no learned savants, and no secret agents to preach insurrection in other states, while defending his own usurpation; besides, his treasury is not in the most brilliant and flourishing situation, and the crew of our white revolutionists are less attached to liberty than to cash.

Our ambassador to the United States, General Turreaux, is far from being contented with our friend, the President Jefferson, whose patriotic notions have not yet soared to the level of our patriotic transactions. He refused both to prevent the marriage of Jerome Bonaparte with a female American citizen, and to detain her after her marriage when her husband returned to Europe. To our continual representation against the liberties which the American newspapers take with our government, with our Emperor, with our imperial family, and with our imperial ministers, the answer has always been, "Prosecute the libeller, and as soon as he is convicted he will be punished." This tardy and *negative* justice is so opposite to our expeditious and summary mode of proceeding, of punishing first and trying afterwards, that it must be both humiliating and offensive. In return, when the Americans have complained to Turreaux against the piracy of our privateers, he has sent them here to seek redress, where they also will, to their cost, discover that in *civil* cases our *justice* has not the same rapid march as when it is a question of arresting or transporting suspected persons, or of tormenting, shooting or guillotining a pretended spy, or supposed conspirator.

Had the peace of Europe continued, Bernadotte was the person selected by Bonaparte and Talleyrand as our representative in America; because we then intended *to strike*, and not to negotiate. But during the present embroiled state of Europe, an intriguer was more necessary there than either a warrior or a politician. A man who has passed through all the mire of our own Revolution, who has been in the secrets, and an accomplice of all our factions, is undoubtedly a useful instrument where factions are to be created and directed, where wealth is designed for pillage, and a state for overthrow. General Turreaux is, therefore, in his place, and at his proper post, as our ambassador in America.

This son of a valet of the late Duke of Bouillon, Turreaux called himself before the Revolution Chevalier de Grambouville, and was, in fact, a *chevalier d'industrie* (a swindler), who supported himself by gambling and cheating. An associate of Beurnonville, Barras and other vile characters, he with them joined the colours of rebellion, and served under the former in 1792, in the army of the Moselle, first as a volunteer, and afterwards as an aide-de-camp. In a speech at the Jacobin Club at Quesnoy, on the 20th of November, 1792, he made a motion—"That, throughout the whole republican army, all hats should be prohibited, and red caps substituted in their place : and, that not only portable guillotines, but *portable Jacobin clubs*, should accompany the soldiers of Liberty and Equality."

A cousin of his was a member of the National Convention, and one of those called *Mountaineers*, or sturdy partisans of Marat and Robespierre. It was to the influence of this cousin, that he was indebted, first for a commission as an adjutant-general, and afterwards for his promotion to a general of brigade. In 1793, he was ordered to march under the command of Santerre, to La Vendée, where he shared in the defeat of the Republicans at Vihiers. At the engagement near Roches d'Erigne he commanded, for the first time, a separate column, and the capacity and abilities which he displayed on that occasion were such as might have been expected from a man who had passed the first thirty years of his life in brothels and gambling-houses. So *pleasant* were his dispositions, that almost the whole army narrowly escaped having been thrown and pushed into the River Loire. The battle of Doué was the only one in which he had a share, where the Republicans were not routed; but some few days afterwards, near Coron, all the troops under him were cut to pieces, and he was himself wounded.

The confidence of his friends, the Jacobins, increased, however, in proportion to his disasters, and he was, in 1794, after the superior number of the Republican soldiers had forced the remnants of the Royalists to evacuate what was properly called La Vendée, appointed a commander-in-chief. He had now an opportunity to display his infamy and barbarity. Having established his headquarters at Nantes, where he was safe, amidst the massacres of women and children ordered by his friend Carrière, he commanded the Republican army to enter La Vendée in twelve columns, preceded by fire and sword; and within four weeks, one of the most populous departments of France, to the extent and circumference of sixty leagues, was laid waste—not a house, not a cottage, not a tree was spared, all was reduced to ashes : and the unfortunate inhabitants who had not perished amid the ruin of their dwellings, were shot or stabbed while attempting to save themselves from the common conflagration. On the 22nd of January, 1794, he wrote to the Committee of Public Safety of the National Convention: "Citizen Representatives! A country of sixty leagues extent, I have the *happiness* to inform you, is now a perfect desert; not a dwelling, not a bush, but is reduced to ashes : and of one hundred and eighty thousand worthless inhabitants, not a soul breathes any longer. Men and women, old men and children, have all experienced the national vengeance, and are no more. It was a *pleasure* to a true Republican to see upon the bayonets of each of our *brave* Republicans the children of traitors, or their heads. According to the lowest calculation, *I have despatched*, within three months, two hundred thousand individuals of both sexes, and of all ages. *Vive la République ! ! !*" In the works of Prudhomme and our republican writers, are inserted hundreds of letters, still more cruelly extravagant, from this *ci-devant* friend of Liberty and Equality, and at present faithful subject, and grand officer of the Legion of Honour, of His Imperial Majesty Napoleon the First.

After the death of Robespierre, Turreaux, then a governor at Belleisle, was arrested as a terrorist, and shut up at du Plessis until the general amnesty released him in 1795. During his imprisonment he amused himself with writing the memoirs of the war of La Vendée, in which he tried to prove that all his barbarities had been perpetrated for the sake of humanity, and to save the lives of Republicans. He had also the modesty to announce that, as a military work, his production would be equally interesting as those of a Folard and Guibert. These memoirs, however, proved nothing but that he was equally ignorant and wicked, presumptuous and ferocious.

During the reign of the Directory he was rather discarded, or only employed as a kind of recruiting officer to hunt young conscripts, but in 1800, Bonaparte gave him a command in the army of reserve; and in 1802, another in the army of the interior. He then became one of the most assiduous and cringing courtiers at the Emperor's levées; while in the Empress's drawing-room he assumed his former air and *ton* of a chevalier, in hopes of imposing upon those who did not remember the nickname which his soldiers gave him ten years before, of Chevalier of the Guillotine.

At a ball of the Bonaparte family to which he was invited, the Emperor took the fancy to dance with his step-daughter, Madame Louis. He therefore unhooked his sword, which he handed to a young colonel, d'Avry, standing by his side. This colonel, who had been a page at the Court of Louis XVI., knew that it would have been against etiquette, and even unbecoming of him, to act as a valet to Napoleon while there were valets in the room; he therefore retreated, looking round for a servant. "Oh!" said the Emperor, "I see that I am mistaken; here, generals," continued he (addressing himself to half-a-dozen, with whose independent principles and *good breeding* he was acquainted), "take this sword during my dance." They all pushed forward, but Turreaux and La Grange, another general and intriguer, were foremost: the latter, however, received the preference. On the next day, d'Avry was ordered *upon service* to Cayenne.

Turreaux has acquired by his *patriotic* deeds in La Vendée a fortune of seven millions of livres —£292,000. He has the highest opinion of his own capacity, while a moment's conversation will inform a man of sense that he is only a conceited fool. As to his political transactions, he has by his side, as a secretary, a man of the name of Petry, who has received a diplomatic education, and does not want either subtlety or parts; and on him, no doubt, is thrown the drudgery of business. During a European war, Turreaux's post is of little relative consequence; but should Napoleon Bonaparte live to dictate another general pacification, the United States will be exposed, on their frontiers or in their interior, to the same outrages their commercial navy now experiences on the main.

LETTER LII

PARIS, *September*, 1805.

MY LORD,—A general officer, who has just arrived from Italy, has assured me that, so far from Bonaparte's subjects on the other side of the Alps being contented and attached to his person and government, were a victorious Austrian army to enter the plains of Lombardy a general insurrection would be the consequence. During these last nine years the inhabitants have not enjoyed a moment's tranquillity or safety. Every relation or favourite whom Napoleon wished to provide for, or to enrich, he has saddled upon them as in free quarters; and since 1796, when they first had the *honour* of our Emperor's acquaintance, they have paid more in taxes, in forced loans, requisitions and extortions of every description, than their ancestors or themselves had paid during the one hundred and ninety-six preceding years.

Such is the public spirit, and such have been the sufferings of the people in the *ci-devant* Lombardy: in Piedmont they are still worse off. Having more national character and more fidelity towards their Sovereign than their neighbours, they are also more cruelly treated. Their governor, General Menou, has caused most of the departments to be declared under martial law, and without right to claim the protection of our *happy* constitution. In every city or town are organised special tribunals, the progeny of our revolutionary tribunals, against the sentences of which no appeal can be made, though these sentences are always capital ones. Before these, suspicion is evidence, and an imprudent word is subject to the same punishment as a murderous deed. Murmur is regarded as mutiny, and he who complains is shot as a conspirator.

There exist only two ways for the wretched Piedmontese to escape these legal assassinations. They must either desert their country or sacrifice a part of their property. In the former case, if retaken, they are condemned as emigrants; and in the latter they incur the risk that those to whom they have already given a part of their possessions, will also require the remainder, and, having obtained it, to enjoy in security the spoil will send them to the tribunals and to death. Menou has a fixed tariff for his protection, regulated according to the riches of each person; and the tax-gatherers collect these arbitrary contributions with the regular ones, so little pains are taken to conceal or to disguise these robberies.

Menou, by turns a nobleman and a *sans-culotte*, a Christian and a Mussulman, is wicked and profligate, not from the impulse of the moment or of any sudden gust of passion, but coldly and deliberately. He calculates with *sang-froid* the profit and the risk of every infamous action he proposes to commit, and determines accordingly. He owed some riches and the rank of a major-general to the bounty of Louis XVI., but when he considered the immense value of the revolutionary plunder, called national property, and that those who confiscated could also promote, he did not hesitate what party to take. A traitor is generally a coward; he has everywhere experienced defeats; he was defeated by his Royalist countrymen in 1793, by his Mahometan sectaries in 1800, and by your countrymen in 1801.

Besides his Turkish wife, Menou has in the same house with her one Italian and two French girls, who live openly with him, but who are obliged to keep themselves by selling their influence and protection, and, perhaps, sometimes even their personal favours. He has also in his hotel several gambling-tables, where those who are too bashful to address themselves to himself or his mistresses may deposit their donations, and if they are thought sufficient, the hint is taken and their business done. He never pays any debts and never buys anything for ready-money, and all persons of his suite, or appertaining to his establishment, have the same privilege. Troublesome creditors are recommended to the care of the special tribunals, which also find means to reduce the obstinacy of those refractory merchants or traders who refuse giving any credit. All the money he extorts or obtains is brought to this capital and laid out by his agents in purchasing estates, which, from his advanced age and weak constitution, he has little prospect of long enjoying. He is a grand officer of Bonaparte's Legion of Honour, and has a long claim to that distinction, because as early as on the 25th of June, 1790, he made a motion in the National Assembly to suppress all former Royal Orders in France, and to create in their place only a national one. Always an incorrigible flatterer, when Napoleon proclaimed himself Ali the Mussulman, Menou professed himself Abdallah the believer in the Alcoran.

The late vice-president of the Italian Republic, Melzi-Eril, is now in complete disgrace with his Sovereign, Napoleon the First. If persons of rank and property would read through the list of those, their equals by birth and wealth, who, after being seduced by the sophistry of impostors, dishonoured and exposed themselves by joining in the Revolution, they might see that none of them have escaped insults, many have suffered death, and all have been, or are, vile slaves, at the mercy of the whip of some upstart beggar, and trampled upon by men started up from the mud, of lowest birth and basest morals. If their revolutionary mania were not incurable, this truth and this evidence would retain them within their duty, so corresponding with their real interest, and prevent them from being any longer borne along by a current of infamy and danger, and preserve them from being lost upon quicksands or dashed against rocks.

The conduct and fate of the Italian nobleman and Spanish grandee, Melzi-Eril, has induced me to make these reflections. Wealthy as well as elevated, he might have passed his life in uninterrupted tranquillity, enjoying its comforts without experiencing its vicissitudes, with the esteem of his contemporaries and without reproach from posterity or from his own conscience. Unfortunately for him, a journey into this country made him acquainted both with our *philosophers* and with our *philosophical* works; and he had neither natural capacity to distinguish errors from reality, nor judgment enough to perceive that what appeared improving and charming in theory, frequently became destructive and improper when attempted to be put into practice. Returned to his own country, his acquired half-learning made him wholly dissatisfied with his government, with his religion, and with himself. In our Revolution he thought that he saw the first approach towards the perfection of the human species, and that it would soon make mankind as good and as regenerated in society as was promised in books. With our own regenerators he extenuated the crimes which sullied their work from its first page, and declared them even necessary to make the conclusion so much the more complete. When, therefore, Bonaparte, in 1796, entered the capital of Lombardy, Melzi was among the first of the Italian nobility who hailed him as a deliverer.

The numerous vexations and repeated pillage of our government, generals, commissaries and soldiers, did not abate his zeal nor alter his opinion. "The faults and sufferings of individuals," he said, "are nothing to the goodness of the cause, and do not impair the utility of the whole." To him, everything the Revolution produced was the best: the murder of thousands and the ruin of millions were, with him, nothing compared with the benefit the universe would one day derive from the principles and instruction of our armed and unarmed philosophers. In recompense for so much complacency, and such great patriotism, Bonaparte appointed him, in 1797, a plenipotentiary from the Cisalpine Republic to the Congress at Rastadt; and, in 1802, a vice-president of the Italian Republic.

As Melzi was a sincere and disinterested republican fanatic, he did not much approve of the strides Bonaparte made towards a sovereignty that annihilated the sovereignty of his sovereign people. In a conference, however, with Talleyrand, at Lyons, in February, 1802, he was convinced that this age was not yet ripe for all the improvements our philosophers intended to confer on it: and that, to prevent it from retrograding to the point where it was found by our Revolution, it was necessary that it should be ruled by enlightened men, such as he and Bonaparte, to whom he advised him by all means never to give the least hint about liberty and equality. Our minister ended his fraternal counsel with obliging Melzi to sign a stipulation for a yearly sum, as a douceur for the place he occupied.

The sweets of power shortly caused Melzi to forget both the tenets of his philosophy and his schemes of regeneration. He trusted so much to the promises of Bonaparte and Talleyrand that he believed himself destined to reign for life, and was, therefore, not a little surprised when he was ordered by Napoleon the First to descend and salute Eugenius de Beauharnais as the deputy Sovereign of the Sovereign King of Italy. He was not philosopher enough to conceal his chagrin, and bowed with such a bad grace to the new Viceroy that it was visible he would have preferred seeing in that situation an Austrian Archduke as a governor-general. To soften his disappointment, Bonaparte offered to make him a Prince, and with that rank indemnify him for breaking the promises given at Lyons, where it is known that the influence of Melzi, more than the intrigues of Talleyrand, determined the Italian Consulta in the choice of a president.

Immediately after Bonaparte's return to France, Melzi left Milan, and retired to an estate in Tuscany; from that place he wrote to Talleyrand a letter full of reproach, and concluded by asking leave to pass the remainder of his days in Spain among his relatives. An answer was presented him by an officer of Bonaparte's Gendarmes d'Élite, in which he was forbidden to quit Italy, and ordered to return with the officer to Milan, and there occupy his office of Arch-Chancellor, to which he had been nominated. Enraged at such treatment, he endeavoured to kill himself with a dose of poison, but his attempt did not succeed. His health was, however, so much injured by it that it is not supposed he can live long. What a lesson for reformers and innovators!

LETTER LIII

Paris, *September*, 1805.

My Lord,—A ridiculous affair lately occasioned a great deal of bustle among the members of our foreign diplomatic corps. When Bonaparte demanded for himself and for his wife the title of Imperial Majesty, and for his brothers and sisters that of Imperial Highness, he also insisted on the salutation of a Serene Highness being given to his Arch-Chancellor, Cambacérès, and his Arch-Treasurer, Le Brun. The political consciences of the independent representatives of independent Continental Princes immediately took the alarm at the latter innovation, as the appellation of Serene Highness has never hitherto been bestowed on persons who had not princely rank. They complained to Talleyrand, they *petitioned* Bonaparte, and they even despatched couriers to their respective Courts. The minister smiled, the Emperor cursed, and their own Cabinets deliberated. All routs, all assemblies, all circles, and all balls were at a stop. Cambacérès applied to his Sovereign to support his pretensions, as connected with his own dignity; and the diplomatic corps held forward their dignity as opposing the pretensions of Cambacérès. In this dilemma Bonaparte ordered all the ambassadors, ministers, envoys, and agents *en masse* to the castle of the Tuileries. After hearing, with apparent patience, their arguments in favour of established etiquette and customs, he remained inflexible, upon the ground that he, as master, had a right to confer what titles he chose within his own dominions on his own subjects; and that those foreigners who refused to submit to his regulations might return to their own country. This plain explanation neither effecting a conversion nor making any impression, he grew warm, and left the refractory diplomatists with these remarkable words: "Were I to create my Mameluke Rostan a King, both you and your masters should acknowledge him in that rank."

After this conference most of their Excellencies were seized with terror and fear, and would, perhaps, have subscribed to the commands of our Emperor had not some of the *wisest* among them proposed, and obtained the consent of the rest, to apply once more to Talleyrand, and purchase by some douceur his assistance in this great business. The heart of our minister is easily softened; and he assented, upon certain conditions, to lay the whole before his Sovereign in such a manner that Cambacérès should be made a Prince as well as a Serene Highness.

It is said that Bonaparte was not easily persuaded to

this measure, and did not consent to it before the minister remarked that his condescension in this insignificant opposition to his will would proclaim his moderation and generosity, and empower him to insist on obedience when matters of the greatest consequence should be in question or disputed. Thus our regicide Cambacérès owes his princely title to the shallow intrigues of the agents of legitimate Sovereigns. Their nicety in talking of *innovations* with regard to him, after they had without difficulty hailed a *sans-culotte* an Emperor, and other *sans-culottes* Imperial Highnesses, was as absurd as improper. Report, however, states, what is very probable, that they were merely the duped tools of Cambacérès' ambition and vanity, and of Talleyrand's corruption and cupidity.

Cambacérès expected to have been elevated to a Prince on the same day that he was made a Serene Highness: but Joseph Bonaparte represented to his brother that too many other princedoms would diminish the respect and value of the princedoms of the Bonaparte family. Cambacérès knew that Talleyrand had some reason at that period to be discontented with Joseph, and, therefore, asked his advice how to get made a Prince against the wishes of this Grand Elector. After some consideration, the minister replied that he was acquainted with one way, which would, with his support, certainly succeed: but it required a million of livres to set the wheels in motion, and keep them going afterwards. The hint was taken, and an agreement signed for one million, payable on the day when the princely patent should be delivered to the Arch-Chancellor.

Among the mistresses provided by our minister for the members of the foreign diplomatic corps, Madam B———s is one of the ablest in the way of intrigue. She was instructed to alarm her *bon ami*, the Bavarian minister, Cetto, who is always bustling and pushing himself forward in the *grand* questions of etiquette. A fool rather than a rogue, and an intriguer while he thinks himself a negotiator, he was happy to have this occasion to prove his penetrating genius and astonishing information. A convocation of the diplomatic corps was therefore called, and the suggestions of Cetto were regarded as an inspiration, and approved of, with a resolution to persevere unanimously. At their first audience with Talleyrand on this subject, he seemed to incline in their favour; but, as soon as he observed how much they showed themselves interested about this trifling punctilio, it occurred to him that they, as well as Cambacérès, might in some way or other reward the service he intended to perform. Madame B———s was again sent for; and she once more advised her lover, who again advised his colleagues. Their scanty purses were opened, and a subscription entered into, for a very valuable diamond, which, with the million of the Arch-Chancellor, gave satisfaction to all parties; and even Joseph Bonaparte was reconciled, upon the consideration that Cambacérès has no children, and that, therefore, the Prince will expire with the Grand Officer of State.

Cambacérès, though before the Revolution a nobleman of a parliamentary family, was so degraded and despised for his unnatural and beastly propensities, that to see him in the ranks of rebellion was not unexpected. Born in Languedoc, his countrymen were the first to suffer from his revolutionary proceedings, and reproached him as one of the most active instruments of persecution against the clergy of Toulouse, and as one of the causes of all the blood that flowed in consequence. A coward as well as a traitor, after the death of Louis XVI. he never dared ascend the tribune of the National Convention, but always gave a silent vote to all the atrocious laws proposed and carried by Marat, Robespierre and their accomplices. It was in 1795, when the Reign of Terror had ceased, that he first displayed his zeal for anarchy, and his hatred to royalty; his contemptible and disgusting vices were, however, so publicly reprobated, that even the Directory dared not nominate him a minister of justice, a place for which he intrigued in vain, from 1796 to 1799; when Bonaparte, either not so scrupulous, or setting himself above public opinion, caused him to be called to the Consulate ; which, in 1802, was ensured him for life, but exchanged, in 1804, for the office of an Arch-Chancellor.

He is now worth thirty millions of livres—£1,250,000 — all *honestly* obtained by his revolutionary industry. Besides a Prince, a Serene Highness, an Arch-Chancellor, a grand officer of the Legion of Honour, he is also a *Knight of the Prussian Black Eagle!* For his brother, who was for a long time an emigrant clergyman, and whom he then renounced as a fanatic, he has now procured the Archbishopric of Rouen and a Cardinal's hat. His Eminence is also a grand officer of the Legion of Honour in France, and a Pope *in petto* at Rome.

LETTER LIV

Paris, *September*, 1805.

My Lord,—No Sovereign Prince has more incurred the hatred of Bonaparte than the present King of Sweden; and I have heard from good authority that our Government spares neither bribes nor intrigues to move the tails of those factions which were dissolved, but not crushed, after the murder of Gustavus III. The Swedes are generally brave and loyal, but their history bears witness that they are easily misled; all their grand achievements are their own, and the consequences of their national spirit and national valour, while all their disasters have been effected by the influence of foreign gold and of foreign machinations. Had they not been the dupes of the plots and views of the Cabinets of Versailles and St. Petersburg their country might have been as powerful in the nineteenth century as it was in the seventeenth.

That Gustavus IV. both knew the danger of Europe and indicated the remedy, His Majesty's notes, as soon as he came of age, presented by the able and loyal minister Bildt to the Diet of Ratisbon, evince. Had they been more attended to during 1798 and 1799, Bonaparte would not, perhaps, have now been so great, but the Continent would have remained more free and more independent. They were the first causes of our Emperor's official anger against the Cabinet of Stockholm.

When, however, His Swedish Majesty entered into the Northern league, his ambassador, Baron Ehrensward, was for some time treated here with no insults distinct or different from those to which all foreign diplomatic agents have been accustomed during the present reign; but when he demanded reparation for the piracies committed during the last war by our privateers on the commerce of his nation, the tone was changed; and when his Sovereign, in 1803, was on a visit to his father-in-law, the Elector of Baden, and there preferred the agreeable company of the unfortunate Duke of Enghien to the society of our minister, Baron Ehrensward never entered Napoleon's diplomatic circle or Madame Napoleon's drawing-room without hearing rebukes and experiencing disgusts. One day, when more than usually attacked, he said, on leaving the apartment, to another ambassador, and in the hearing of Duroc, "that it required more real courage to encounter with dignity and self-command unbecoming provocations, which the person who gave them knew could not be resented, than to brave a death which the mouths of cannon vomit or the point of bayonets inflict." Duroc reported to his master what he heard, and but for Talleyrand's interference, the Swedish ambassador would, on the same night, have been lodged in the Temple. Orders were already given to that purpose, but were revoked.

This Baron Ehrensward, who is also a general in the service of his country, has almost from his youth passed his time at Courts: first in his own country, and afterwards in Spain, where he resided twelve years as our ambassador. Frank as a soldier, but also polite as a courtier, he was not a little surprised at the new etiquette of our new Court, and at the endurance of all the members of the diplomatic corps, of whom hardly one had spirit enough to remember that he was the representative of one, at least nominally, independent Prince or State. It must be added that he was the only foreign diplomatist, with Count Markoff, who was not the choice of our Cabinet, and, therefore, was not in our secrets.

As soon as His Swedish Majesty heard of the unexpected and unlawful seizure of the Duke of Enghien, he wrote a letter with his own hand to Bonaparte, which he sent by his adjutant-general, Tawast; but this officer arrived too late, and only in time to hear of the execution of the Prince he intended to save and the indecent expressions of Napoleon when acquainted with the object of his mission. Baron Ehrensward was then recalled, and a Court mourning was proclaimed by Gustavus IV., as well as by Alexander the First, for the lamented victim of the violated laws of nations and humanity. This so enraged our ruler that General Caulincourt (the same who commanded the expedition which crossed the Rhine and captured the Duke of Enghien) was engaged to head and lead fifty other banditti, who were destined *to pass in disguise* into Baden and to bring the King of Sweden a prisoner to this capital. Fortunately His Majesty had some suspicion of the attempt, and removed to a greater distance from our frontiers than Carlsruhe. So certain was our Government of the success of this shameful enterprise, that our chargé d'affaires in Sweden was preparing to engage the discontented and disaffected there for the convocation of a diet and the establishment of a regency.

According to the report in our diplomatic circle, Bonaparte and Talleyrand intended nevermore to release their royal captive when once in their power; but, after forcing him to resign the throne to his son, keep him a prisoner for the remainder of his days, which they would have taken care should not have been long. The Duke of Sudermania was to have been nominated a regent until the majority of the young King, not yet six years of age. The Swedish diets were to recover that influence, or rather that licentiousness, to which Gustavus III., by the revolution of the 19th of August, 1772, put an end. All exiled regicides, or traitors, were to be recalled, and a revolutionary focus organized in the North, equally threatening Russia and Denmark. The dreadful consequences of such an event are incalculable. Thanks to the prudence of His Swedish Majesty, all these schemes evaporated in air.

Not being able to dethrone a Swedish monarch, our Cabinet resolved to partition the Swedish territory, to which effect I am assured that proposals were last summer made to the Cabinets of St. Petersburg, Berlin and Copenhagen. Swedish Finland was stated to have been offered to Russia, Swedish Pomerania to Prussia, and Scania and Blekinge to Denmark ; but the overture was rejected.

The King of Sweden possesses both talents and information superior to most of his contemporaries, and he has surrounded himself with counsellors who, with their experience, make wisdom more firm, more useful, and more valuable. His chancellor, d'Ehrenheim, unites modesty with sagacity ; he is a most able statesman, an accomplished gentleman, and the most agreeable of men. He knows the languages, as well as the constitutions, of every country in Europe, with equal perfection as his native tongue and national code. Had his Sovereign the same ascendency over the European politics as Christina had during the negotiation of the Treaty of Munster, other states would admire, and Sweden be proud of, another Axel Oxenstiern.

Count de Fersen, who also has, and is worthy of, the confidence of his Prince, is a nobleman, the honour and pride of his rank. A colonel before the revolution of the regiment, *Royal Suédois*, in the service of my country, his principles were so well appreciated, that he was entrusted by Louis XVI. and Marie Antoinette, when so many were justly suspected, and served royalty in distress, at the risk of his own existence. This was so much the more generous in him as he was a foreigner, of one of the most ancient families, and one of the richest noblemen in his own country. To him Louis XVIII. is indebted for his life; and he brought consolation to the deserted Marie Antoinette even in the dungeon of the Conciergerie, when a discovery would have been a sentence of death. In 1797, he was appointed by his King plenipotentiary to the Congress of Rastadt, and arrived there just at the time when Bonaparte, after the destruction of happiness in Italy, had resolved on the ruin of liberty in Switzerland, and came there proud of past exploits and big with future schemes of mischief. His reception from the Conqueror of Italy was such as might have been expected by distinguished loyalty from successful rebellion. He was told that the Congress of Rastadt was not his place! and this was true; for what can be common between honour and infamy, between virtue and vice? On his return to Sweden, Count de Fersen was rewarded with the dignity of a Grand Officer of State.

Of another faithful and trusty counsellor of His Swedish Majesty, Baron d'Armfeldt, a panegyric would be pronounced in saying that he was the friend of Gustavus III. From a page to that chevalier of royalty he was advanced to the rank of general; and during the war with Russia, in 1789 and 1790, he fought and bled by the side of his Prince and benefactor. It was to him that his King said, when wounded mortally, by the hand of a regicide, at a masquerade in March, 1792, "Don't be alarmed, my friend! You know as well as myself that all wounds are not dangerous." Unfortunately, his were not of that description.

In the will of this great monarch, Baron d'Armfeldt was nominated one of the guardians of his present Sovereign, and a governor of the capital; but the Duke Regent, who was a weak prince, guided by philosophical adventurers, by Illuminati and Freemasons, most of whom had imbibed the French revolutionary maxims, sent him, in a kind of honourable exile, as an ambassador to Italy. Shortly afterwards, under pretence of having discovered a conspiracy, in which the Baron was implicated, he was outlawed. He then took refuge in Russia, where he was made a general, and as such distinguished himself under Suwarow during the campaign of 1799. He was then recalled to his country, and restored to all his former places and dignities, and has never since ceased to merit and obtain the favour, friendship and approbation of his King. He is said to be one of the Swedish general officers intended to serve in union with the Russian troops expected in Pomerania. Wherever he is employed, I am convinced that he will fight, vanquish, or perish like a hero. Last spring he was offered the place of a lieutenant-general in the Austrian service, which, with regard to salary and emoluments, is greatly superior to what he enjoys in Sweden : he declined it, however, because, with a warrior of his stamp, interest is the last consideration.

LETTER LV

Paris, *September*, 1805.

My Lord,—Believe me, Bonaparte dreads more the liberty of the Press than all other engines—military or political—used by his rivals or foes for his destruction. He is aware of the fatal consequences all former factions suffered from the public exposure of their past crimes and future views; of the reality of their guilt, and of the fallacy of their boasts and promises. He does not doubt but that a faithful account of all the actions and intrigues of his government, its imposition, fraud, duplicity and tyranny, would make a sensible alteration in the public opinion; and that even those who, from motives of patriotism, from being tired of our revolutionary convulsions, or wishing for tranquillity, have been his adherents, might alter their sentiments when they read of enormities which must indicate insecurity, and prove to everyone that he who waded through rivers of blood to seize power will never hesitate about the means of preserving it.

There is not a printing-office, from the banks of the Elbe to the Gulf of Naples, which is not under the direct or indirect inspection of our police-agents; and not a bookseller in Germany, France, Italy, Spain, Portugal, Holland, or Switzerland, publishes a work which, if contrary to our policy or our *fears*, is not either confiscated, or purchased on the day it makes its appearance. Besides our regular emissaries, we have persons travelling from the beginning to the end of the year, to pick up information of what literary productions are printing : of what authors are popular ; of their political opinions and private circumstances. This branch of our *haute police* extends even to your country.

Before the Revolution, we had in this capital only two daily papers, but from 1789 to 1799 never less than thirty, and frequently sixty, journals were daily printed. After Bonaparte had assumed the consular authority, they were reduced to ten. But though these were under a very strict inspection of our minister of police, they were regarded still as too numerous, and have lately been diminished to eight, by the *incorporation* of *Le Clef du Cabinet* and *Le Bulletin de l'Europe* with the *Gazette de France*, a paper of which the infamously famous Barrère is the editor. According to a proposal of Bonaparte, it was lately debated in the Council of State whether it would not be politic to suppress all daily prints, with the sole exception of the *Moniteur*. Fouché and Talleyrand spoke much in favour of this measure of *security*. Real, however, is said to have suggested another plan, which was adopted : and our Government, instead of prohibiting the appearance of our daily papers, has resolved by degrees to purchase them *all*, and to entrust them entirely to the direction of Barrère, who now is consulted in everything concerning books or newspapers.

All circulation of foreign papers is prohibited, until they have previously obtained the *stamp* of approbation from the grand literary censor, Barrère. Any person offending against this law is most severely punished. An American gentleman, of the name of Campbell, was last spring sent to the Temple for lending one of your old daily papers to a person who lodged in the same hotel with him. After an imprisonment of ten weeks he made some pecuniary sacrifices to obtain his liberty, but was carried to Havre, under an escort of gendarmes, put on board a neutral vessel, and forbidden, under pain of death, ever to set his foot on French ground again. An American vessel was, about the same time confiscated at Bordeaux, and the captain and crew imprisoned, because some English books were found on board, in which Bonaparte, Talleyrand, Fouché, and some of our great men were rather ill-treated. The crew have since been liberated, but the captain has been brought here, and is still in the Temple. The vessel and the cargo have been sold as lawful captures, though the captain has proved from the names written in the books that they belonged to a passenger. A young German student in surgery, who came here to improve himself, has been nine months in the same state prison, for having with him a book, printed in Germany during Bonaparte's expedition to Egypt, wherein the chief and the undertaking are ridiculed. His mother, the widow of a clergyman, hearing of the misfortune of her son, came here, and has presented to the Emperor and Empress half-a-dozen petitions, without any effect whatever, and has almost ruined herself and her other children by the expenses of the journey. During a stay of four months she has not yet been able to gain admittance into the Temple, to visit or see her son, who perhaps expired in tortures, or died broken-hearted before she came here.

A dozen copies of a funeral sermon on the Duke of Enghien had found their way here, and were secretly circulated for some time; but at last the police heard of it, and every person who was suspected of having read them was arrested. The number of these unfortunate persons, according to some, amounted to one hundred and thirty, while others say that they were only eighty-four, of whom twelve *died suddenly* in the Temple, and the remainder were transported to Cayenne: upwards of half of them were women, some of the *ci-devant* highest rank among subjects. A Prussian, of the name of Bülow, was shot as a spy in the camp of Boulogne, because in his trunk was an English book, with the lives of Bonaparte and of some of his generals. Every day such and other examples of the severity of our Government are related : and foreigners who visit us continue, nevertheless, to be off their guard. They would be less punished had they with them forged bills than printed books or newspapers, in which our imperial family and public functionaries are not treated with *due* respect. Bonaparte is convinced that in every book where he is not spoken of with praise, the intent is to blame him : and such intents or negative guilt never escape with impunity.

As, notwithstanding the endeavours of our Government, we are more fond of foreign prints, and have more confidence in them than in our own, *official* presses have lately been established at Antwerp, at Cologne, and at Mentz, where the *Gazette de Leyden, Hamburg Correspondenten,* and *Journal de Frankfort* are reprinted ; some articles left out, and others inserted in their room. It was intended to reprint also the *Courier de Londres,* but our types, and particularly our paper, would detect the fraud. I have read one of our own *Journal de Frankfort,* in which were extracts from this French paper, printed in your country, which I strongly suspect are of our own manufacture. I am told that several new books, *written by foreigners*, in praise of our present brilliant Government, are now in the presses of those our frontier towns, and will soon be laid before the public as foreign productions.

A clerk of a banking-house had lately the imprudence to mention, during his dinner at the restaurateur's of *Cadran Vert*, on the Boulevards, some doubt of the veracity of an official article in the *Moniteur*. As he left the house he was arrested, carried before Fouché, accused of being an English agent, and before supper-time he was on the road to Rochefort on his way to Cayenne. As soon as the banker Tournon was informed of this *expeditious justice*, as it is called here, he waited on Fouché, who threatened even to transport him if he dared to interfere with the transactions of the police. This banker was himself seized in the spring of last year by a police agent and some gendarmes, and carried into exile forty leagues from this capital, where he remained six months, until a pecuniary douceur procured him a recall. His *crime* was having enquired after General Moreau when in the Temple, and of having left his card there.

LETTER LVI

PARIS, *September*, 1805.

MY LORD,—The Prince of Borghese has lately been appointed a captain of the Imperial Guard of his imperial brother-in-law Napoleon the First, and is now in Germany, making his first campaign. A descendant of a wealthy and ancient Roman family, but born with a weak understanding, he was easily deluded into the ranks of the Revolutionists of his own country, by a Parisian abbé, his instructor and governor, and the gallant of the Princess Borghese, his mother. He was the first secretary of the first Jacobin club established at Rome, in the spring of 1798; and in December of the same year, when the Neapolitan troops invaded the Ecclesiastical States, he, with his present brother-in-law, another hopeful Roman Prince, Santa Cruce, headed the Roman *sans-culottes* in their retreat. To show his love of equality, he had previously served as a common man in a company of which the captain was a fellow that sold cats'-meat and tripe in the streets of Rome, and the lieutenant a scullion of his mother's kitchen. Since imperial aristocracy is now become the order of the day, he is as insupportable for his pride and vanity as he, some years ago, was contemptible for his meanness. He married, in 1803, Madame Le Clerc, who, between the death of a first and a wedding with a second husband—a space of twelve months—had twice been in a fair way to become a mother. Her portion was estimated at eighteen millions of livres— £750,000—a sum sufficient to palliate many *faux pas* in the eyes of a husband more sensible and more delicate than her present *Serene Idiot*, as she styles the Prince of Borghese.

The lady is the favourite sister of Napoleon, the *ablest*, but also the most wicked of the female Bonapartes. She had, almost from her infancy, passed through all the filth of prostitution, debauchery and profligacy before she attained her present elevation; rank, however, has not altered her *morals*, but only procured her the means of indulging in new excesses. Ever since the wedding night the Prince of Borghese has been excluded from her bed; for she declared frankly to him, as well as to her brother, that she would never endure the approach of a man with a bad breath; though many who, from the opportunities they have had of judging, certainly ought to know, pretend that her own breath is not the sweetest in the world. When her husband had marched towards the Rhine, she asked her brother, as a favour, to procure the Prince of Borghese, after a *useless* life, a *glorious* death. This curious demand of a wife was made in Madame Bonaparte's drawing-room, in the presence of fifty persons. "You are always *étourdie*," replied Napoleon, smiling.

If Bonaparte, however, overlooks the intrigues of his sisters, he is not so easily pacified when any reports reach him inculpating the *virtues* of his sisters-in-law. Some gallants of Madame Joseph Bonaparte have already disappeared to return no more, or are wandering in the wilds of Cayenne; but the Emperor is particularly attentive to everything concerning the *morality* of Madame Louis, whose descendants are destined to continue the Bonaparte dynasty. Two officers, after being cashiered, were, with two of Madame Louis' maids, shut up last month in the Temple, and have not since been heard of, upon suspicion that the Princess preferred their society to that of her husband.

Louis Bonaparte, whose constitution has been much impaired by his debaucheries, was, last July, advised by his physicians to use the baths at St. Amand. After his wife had accompanied him as far as Lille, she went to visit one of her friends, Madame Ney, the wife of General Ney, who commanded the camp near Montreuil. This lady resided in a castle called Leek, in the vicinity, where dinners, concerts, balls and other festivities, celebrated the arrival of the Princess; and to these the principal officers of the camp were invited. One morning, about an hour after the company had retired to bed, the whole castle was disturbed and alarmed by an uproar in the ante-room of Princess Louis' bed-chamber. On coming to the scene of riot, two officers were found there fighting, and the Princess Louis, more than half undressed, came out and called the sentries on duty to separate the combatants, who were both wounded. This affair occasioned great scandal; and General Ney, after having put the officers under arrest, sent a courier to Napoleon at Boulogne, relating the particulars and demanding His Majesty's orders. It was related and *believed* as a fact that the quarrel originated about two of the maids of the Princess (whose *virtue* was never suspected), with whom the officers were intriguing. The Emperor ordered the culprits to be broken and delivered up to his minister of police, who knew how to proceed. The Princess Louis also received an *invitation* to join her sister-in-law, Madame Murat, then in the camp at Boulogne, and to remain under her care until her husband's return from St. Amand.

General Murat was then at Paris, and his lady was merely on a visit to her imperial brother, who made her responsible for Madame Louis, whom he severely reprimanded for the misconduct of her maids. The bedrooms of the two sisters were on the same floor. One night, Princess Louis thought she heard the footsteps of a person on the staircase, not like those of a female, and afterwards the door of Madame Murat's room opened softly. This occurrence deprived her of all desire to sleep; and curiosity, or perhaps revenge, excited her to remove her doubts concerning the *virtue* of her guardian. In about an hour afterwards, she stole into Madame Murat's bedroom, by the way of their sitting-room, the door in the passage being bolted. Passing her hand over the pillow, she almost pricked herself with the strong beard of a man, and screaming out, awoke her sister, who enquired what she could want at such an unusual hour. "I believe," replied the Princess, "my room is haunted. I have not shut my eyes, and intended to ask for a place by your side, but I find it is already engaged."—"My maid always sleeps with me when my husband is absent," said Madame Murat.—"It is very rude of your maid to go to bed with her mistress without first shaving herself," said the Princess, and left the room. The next morning an explanation took place; the ladies understood each other, and each, during the remaining part of her husband's absence, had for consolation *a maid* for a bed-fellow. Madame Murat also convinced the Emperor that his suspicions with regard to the Princess Louis were totally unfounded; and he, with some precious presents, indemnified her for his harsh treatment.

It is reported that the two maids of the Princess Louis, when before Fouché, first denied all acquaintance with the officers; but, being threatened with tortures, they signed a *procès verbal*, acknowledging their guilt. This valuable and *authentic* document the minister sent by an extra courier to the Emperor, who showed it to his step-daughter. Her generosity is proverbial here, and therefore nobody is surprised that she has given a handsome sum of money to the parents of her maids, who had in vain applied to see their children; Fouché having told them that *affairs of state* still required their confinement. One of them, Mariothe, has been in the service of the Princess ever since her marriage, and is known to possess all her confidence; though during that period of four years she has twice been in a state of pregnancy, through the condescending attention of her princely master.

LETTER LVII

PARIS, *September*, 1805.

MY LORD,—When preparations were made for the departure of our army of England for Germany, it excited both laughter and murmuring among the troops. Those who had always regarded the conquest of England as impracticable in present circumstances laughed, and those who had in their imagination shared the wealth of your country, showed themselves vexed at their disappointment. To keep them in good spirits, the company of the theatre of the Vaudevilles were ordered from hence to Boulogne, and several plays composed for the occasion were performed, in which the Germans were represented as defeated, and the English begging for peace on their knees, which the Emperor of the French grants upon condition that one hundred guineas ready-money should be paid to each of his soldiers and sailors. Every corps in its turn was admitted gratis to witness this exhibition of the end of all their labours; and you can form no idea what effect it produced, though you are not a stranger to our fickle and inconsiderate character. Ballads, with the same predictions and the same promises, were written and distributed among the soldiers, and sung by women sent by Fouché to the coast. As all productions of this sort were as usual liberally rewarded by the Emperor, they poured in from all parts of his empire.

Three poets and authors for the theatre of the Vaudevilles, Barré, Radet and Desfontaines, each received two hundred napoléons d'or for their common production of a ballad called, "*Les Adieux d'un Grenadier au Camp de Boulogne.*" From this I have extracted the following sample, by which you may judge of the remainder:—

> Le tambour bat ; il faut partir :
>   Ailleurs on nous appelle ;
> Et de lauriers, il va s'offrir
>   Une moisson nouvelle.
> Si là-bas ils sont assez fous
>   Pour troubler l'Allemagne,
> Tant pis pour eux, tant mieux pour nous ;
>   Allons : vite en campagne !
>
> Là par ses exploits éclatans
>   On connoît notre armée ;
> C'est là qu'elle est depuis longtemps
>   À vaincre accoutumée ;
> C'est là que nos braves guerriers
>   Vont triompher d'emblée ;
> C'est le pays où les lauriers
>   Sont en coupe réglée.
>
> Adieu, mon cher petit jardin,
>   Ma cabane jolie,

Toi que j'ai planté de ma main,
   Et toi que j'ai bâtie !
Puisqu'il faut prendre mon mousquet
   Et quitter ma chaumière,
Je m'en vais planter le piquet
   Par delà la frontière.

Adieu, poules, pigeons, lapins,
   Et ma chatte gentille,
Autour de moi tous les matins
   Rassemblés en famille !
Toi, mon chien, ne me quitte pas !
   Compagnon de ma *gloire*,
Tu dois toujours suivre mes pas :
   Ton nom est *la Victoire*.

SANS ADIEU, péniches, bateaux,
   Prames et cannonières,
Qui *deviez* porter sur les eaux
   Nos braves militaires !
Vous, ne soyez pas si contens,
   Messieurs de la Tamise :
Seulement pour quelques instans
   La partie est remise !

THE GRENADIER'S ADIEU

TO THE CAMP AT BOULOGNE

The drum is beating, we must march,
   We're summon'd to another field,
A field that to our conq'ring swords
   Shall soon a laurel harvest yield.
If English folly light the torch
   Of war in Germany again—
The loss is theirs—the gain is ours—
   March ! march ! commence the bright campaign.

There, only by their glorious deeds
    Our chiefs and gallant bands are known;
There, often have they met their foes,
    And victory was all their own:—
There, hostile ranks, at our approach,
    Prostrate beneath our feet shall bow;
There, smiling conquest waits to twine
    A laurel wreath round every brow.

Adieu, my pretty turf-built hut[1]!
    Adieu, my little garden[1] too!
I made, I deck'd you all myself,
    And I am loth to part with you:
But since my arms I must resume,
    And leave your comforts all behind,
Upon the hostile frontier soon
    My tent shall flutter in the wind.

My pretty fowls and doves, adieu!
    Adieu, my playful cat, to thee!
Who every morning round me came,
    And were my little family.
But thee, my dog, I shall not leave—
    No, thou shalt ever follow me,
Shalt share my toils, shalt share my fame
    For thou art callèd VICTORY.

But no farewell I bid to you,
    Ye prams and boats, which, o'er the wave,

---

1 During the long continuance of the French encampment at Boulogne the troops had formed, as it were, a romantic town of huts. Every hut had a garden surrounding it, kept in neat order and stocked with vegetables and flowers. They had, besides, fowls, pigeons and rabbits; and these, with a cat and a dog, generally formed the little household of every soldier.

Were doom'd to waft to England's shore
  Our hero chiefs, our soldiers brave.
To you, good gentlemen of Thames,
  Soon, soon our visit shall be paid,
Soon, soon your merriment be o'er—
  'Tis but a few short hours delay'd.

As I am writing on the subject of *poetical* agents, I will also say some words of our poetical flatterers, though the same persons frequently occupy both the one office and the other. A man of the name of Richaud, who has sung previously *the glory* of Marat and Robespierre, offered to Bonaparte, on the evening preceding his departure for Strasburg, the following lines; and was in return presented with a purse full of gold, and an order to the minister of the interior, Champagny, to be employed in his offices, until better provided for :—

STANCES
SUR LES BRUITS DE GUERRE AVEC L'AUTRICHE

Rois tant de fois vaincus, O Rois dont l'imprudence
  Menace encore votre vainqueur,
Fixez en ce moment vos regards sur la France,
  Et perdez tout espoir en voyant sa *splendeur*.

Quel orgueil deplorable, insensés que vous êtes,
  Peut donc encore vous abuser?
Tremblez, si votre voix invoque les tempêtes;
  La foudre va partir, mais pour vous écraser.

Et toi Napoléon, s'il faut à la victoire
  Ramener ce peuple guerrier,

Vas ! l'Europe est témoin qu'au laurier de la gloire
 Ton cœur eut préféré le modeste olivier.

Mais du soldat français la valeur irritée
 T'appelle à de nouveaux exploits,
Dis un mot, un seul mot, et Vienne épouvantée
 Va revoir nos drapeaux . . . pour la dernière fois.

STANZAS

ON THE RUMOUR OF A WAR WITH AUSTRIA

Kings who, so often vanquish'd, vainly dare
 Menace the victor that has laid you low—
Look now at France—and view your own despair
 In the majestic splendour of your foe.

What miserable pride, ye foolish kings,
 Still your deluded reason thus misleads?
Provoke the storm—the bolt with lightning wings
 Shall fall—but fall on your devoted heads.

And thou, Napoleon, if thy mighty sword
 Shall for thy people conquer new renown;
Go—Europe shall attest, thy heart preferr'd
 The modest olive to the laurel crown.

But thee, lov'd chief, to new achievements bold
 The aroused spirit of the soldier calls;
Speak!—and Vienna cowering shall behold
 Our banners waving o'er her prostrate walls.

I received four days afterwards, at the circle of Madame Joseph Bonaparte, with all other visitors, a copy of these stanzas. Most of the foreign ambassadors were of the party, and had also a share of this patriotic donation. Count de Cobenzel had prudently absented himself; otherwise, this *delenda* of the Austrian Carthage would have been officially announced to him.

Another poetaster, of the name of Brouet, in a long, dull, disgusting poem, after comparing Bonaparte with all great men of antiquity, and *proving* that he surpasses them all, tells his countrymen that their Emperor is the deputy Divinity upon earth—the mirror of wisdom, a demi-god to whom future ages will erect statues, build temples, burn incense, fall down and adore. A proportionate share of abuse is, of course, bestowed on your nation. He says:

> À Londres on vit briller d'un éclat éphémère
> Le front tout radieux d'un ministre influent ;
> Mais pour faire pâlir l'étoile d'Angleterre,
> Un SOLEIL tout nouveau parut au firmament,
> Et ce soleil du peuple franc
> *Admiré* de l'Europe *entière*
> Sur la terre est nommé BONAPARTE LE GRAND.

For this *delicate* compliment Brouet was made deputy postmaster-general in Italy, and a Knight of the Legion of Honour. It must be granted that, if Bonaparte is fond of flattery, he does not receive it gratis, but pays for it like a real Emperor.

It has lately become the etiquette, not only in our Court circle and official assemblies, but even in fashionable societies of persons who are, or wish to become, Bonaparte's public functionaries, to distribute and have read and applauded these *disinterested* effusions of our poetical geniuses. This fashion occasioned lately a curious blunder, at a tea-party in the hotel of Madame Talleyrand. The same printer who had been engaged by this lady had also been employed by Chenier, or some other poet, to print a short satire against several of our literary ladies, in which Madame de Genlis and Madame de Staël (who has just arrived here from her exile) were, with others, very severely handled. By mistake, a bundle of this production was given to the porter of Madame Talleyrand, and a copy was handed to each visitor, even to Madame de Genlis and Madame de Staël, who took them without noticing their contents. Picard, after reading an act of a new play, was asked by the lady of the house to read this poetic worship of the Emperor of the French. After the two first lines he stopped short, looking round him confused, suspecting a trick had been played upon him. This induced the audience to read what had been given them, and Madame Talleyrand with the rest; who, instead of permitting Picard to continue with another scene of his play, as he had adroitly begun, made the most awkward apology in the world, and by it exposed the ladies still more who were the objects of the satire; which, an hour afterwards, was exchanged for the verses intended for the homage of the Emperor, and the cause of the error was cleared up.

I have read somewhere of a tyrant of antiquity who forced all his subjects to furnish one room of their houses in the best possible manner, according to their circumstances, and to have it consecrated for the reception of his bust, before which, under pain of death, they were commanded to prostrate themselves, morning, noon and night. They were to enter this room, bare-headed and bare-footed, to remain there only on their knees, and to leave it without turning their back towards the sacred representative of their Prince. All laughing, sneezing, coughing, speaking, or even whispering, were capitally prohibited ; but crying was not only permitted, but commanded, when His Majesty was offended, angry or unwell. Should our system of cringing continue progressively to increase as it has done these last three years, we, too, shall very soon have rooms consecrated, and an idol to adore.

LETTER LVIII

PARIS, *September*, 1805.

MY LORD,—Portugal has suffered more from the degraded state of Spain, under the administration of the Prince of Peace, than we yet have gained by it in France. Engaged by her, in 1793, in a war against its inclination and interest, it was not only deserted afterwards, but sacrificed. But for the dictates of the Court of Madrid, supported, perhaps, by some secret influence of the Court of St. James', the Court of Lisbon would have preserved its neutrality, and, though not a well-wisher of the French Republic, never have been counted among her avowed enemies.

In the Peace of 1795, and in the subsequent Treaty of 1796, which transformed the family compact of the French and Spanish Bourbons into a national alliance between France and Spain, there was no question about Portugal. In 1797, indeed, our Government condescended to receive a Portuguese plenipotentiary, but merely for the purpose of plundering his country of some millions of money, and to insult it by shutting up its representative as a state prisoner in the Temple. Of this violation of the laws of civilized nations, Spain never complained, nor had Portugal any means to avenge it. After four years of negotiation, and an expenditure of thirty millions, the imbecile Spanish premier supported demands made by our Government, which, if assented to, would have left Her Most Faithful Majesty without any territory in Europe, and without any place of refuge in America. Circumstances not permitting your country to send any but pecuniary succours, Portugal would have become an easy prey to the united Spanish and French forces, had the marauders agreed about the partition of the spoil. Their disunion, the consequence of their avidity, saved it from ruin, but not from pillage. A province was ceded to Spain, the banks and the navigation of a river to France, and fifty millions to the private purse of the Bonaparte family.

It might have been supposed that such renunciations, and such offerings, would have satiated ambition, as well as cupidity; but though the Cabinet of Lisbon was in peace with the Cabinet of St. Cloud, the pretensions and encroachments of the latter left the former no rest. While pocketing tributes it required commercial monopolies, and when its commerce was favoured, it demanded sea-ports to ensure the security of its trade. Its pretensions rose in proportion to the condescensions of the State it oppressed. With the money and the value of the diamonds which

Portugal has paid in loans, in contributions, in requisitions, in donations, in tributes, and in presents, it might have supported, during ten years, an army of one hundred thousand men; and could it then have been worse situated than it has been since, and is still at this moment?

But the manner of extorting, and the individuals employed to extort, were more humiliating to its dignity and independence than the extortions themselves were injurious to its resources. The first revolutionary ambassador Bonaparte sent thither evinced both his ingratitude and his contempt.

Few of our many upstart generals have more illiberal sentiments, and more vulgar and insolent manners, than General Lasnes. The son of a publican and a smuggler, he was a smuggler himself in his youth, and afterwards a postillion, a dragoon, a deserter, a coiner, a Jacobin, and a terrorist; and he has, with all the meanness and brutality of these different *trades*, a kind of native impertinence and audacity which shocks and disgusts. He seems to say, "I am a villain. I know that I am so, and I am proud of being so. To obtain the rank I possess I have respected no human laws, and I bid defiance to all Divine vengeance. I might be murdered or hanged, but it is impossible to degrade me. On a gibbet or in the palace of a prince, seized by the executioner or dining with sovereigns, I am,

I will, and I must, always remain the same. Infamy cannot debase me, nor is it in the power of grandeur to exalt me." General, ambassador, field-marshal, first consul, or emperor, Lasnes will always be the same polluted, but daring individual; a stranger to remorse and repentance, as well as to honour and virtue. Where Bonaparte sends a banditto of such a stamp, he has resolved on destruction.

A kind of temporary disgrace was said to have occasioned Lasnes' first mission to Portugal. When commander of the consular guard, in 1802, he had appropriated to himself a sum of money from the regimental chest, and, as a punishment, was *exiled as an ambassador*, as he said himself. His resentment against Bonaparte he took care to pour out on the Regent of Portugal. Without enquiring or caring about the etiquette of the Court of Lisbon, he brought the *sans-culotte* etiquette of the Court of the Tuileries with him, and determined to fraternize with a foreign and legitimate Sovereign, as he had done with his own *sans-culotte* friend and First Consul; and, what is the more surprising, he carried his point. The Prince Regent not only admitted him to the royal table, but stood sponsor to his child by a wife who had been two years his mistress before he was divorced from his first spouse, and with whom the Prince's consort, a Bourbon princess and a daughter of a king, was also obliged to associate.

Avaricious as well as unprincipled, he pursued, as an ambassador, his former business of a smuggler, and, instead of being ashamed of a discovery, proclaimed it publicly, deserted his post, was not reprimanded in France, but was, without apology, received back again in Portugal. His conduct afterwards could not be surprising. He *only* insisted that some faithful and able ministers should be removed, and others appointed in their place, more complaisant and less honest.

New plans of Bonaparte, however, delivered Portugal from this plague; but what did it obtain in return?--another grenadier ambassador, less brutal but more cunning, as abandoned but more dissimulating.

General Junot is the son of a corn-chandler near the corn-market of this capital, and was a shopman to his father in 1789. Having committed some pilfering, he was turned out of the parental dwelling, and therefore lodged himself as an inmate of the Jacobin club. In 1792, he entered as a soldier in a regiment of the army marching against the county of Nice; and, in 1793, he served before Toulon, where he became acquainted with Bonaparte, whom he, in January, 1794, assisted in despatching the unfortunate Toulonese; and with whom, also in the autumn of the same year, he, therefore, was arrested as a terrorist.

In 1796, when commander-in-chief, Bonaparte made

Junot his aide-de-camp; and in that capacity he accompanied him, in 1798, to Egypt. There, as well as in Italy, he fought bravely, but had no particular opportunity of distinguishing himself. He was not one of those select few whom Napoleon brought with him to Europe in 1799, but returned first to France in 1801, when he was nominated a general of division and commander of this capital, a place he resigned last year to General Murat.

His despotic and cruel behaviour while commander of Paris made him not much regretted. Fouché lost in him, indeed, an able support, but none of us here ever experienced from him justice, much less protection. As with all other of our modern public functionaries, without money nothing was obtained from him. It required as much for not doing any harm as if, in renouncing his usual vexatious oppressions, he had conferred benefits. He was much suspected of being, with Fouché, the patron of a gang of street-robbers and housebreakers, who, in the winter of 1803, infested this capital, and who, when finally discovered, were sereened from justice and suffered to escape punishment.

I will tell you what I personally have seen of him. Happening one evening to enter the rooms at Frascati, where the gambling-tables are kept, I observed him, undressed, out of regimentals, in company with a young man, who afterwards avowed himself an aide-de-camp of this general, and who was playing with *rouleaux* of louis d'or, supposed to contain fifty each, at Rouge et Noir. As long as he lost, which he did several times, he took up the *rouleau* on the table and gave another from his pocket. At last he won, when he asked the bankers to look at their loss and count the money in his *rouleau* before they paid him. On opening it, they found it contained one hundred bank-notes of one thousand livres each—£4,125 folded in a manner to resemble the form and size of louis d'or. The bankers refused to pay, and applied to the company whether they were not in the right to do so, after so many *rouleaux* had been changed by the person who now required such an unusual sum in such an unusual manner. Before any answer could be given, Junot interfered, asking the bankers whether they knew who he was. Upon their answering in the negative, he said, "I am General Junot, the commander of Paris, and this officer who has won the money is my aide-de-camp; and I insist upon your paying him this instant, if you do not wish to have your bank confiscated and your persons arrested." They refused to part with money which they protested was not their own, and most of the individuals present joined them in their resistance. "You are altogether a set of scoundrels and sharpers," interrupted Junot; "your business shall soon be done." So saying, he seized all the money on the table, and a kind of boxing-match ensued between him and the bankers, in which he, being a tall and strong man, got the better of them. The tumult, however, brought in the guard, whom he ordered, *as their chief*, to carry to prison sixteen persons he pointed out. Fortunately I was not of the number—I say fortunately, for I have heard that most of them remained imprisoned six months before this *delicate* affair was cleared up and settled. In the meantime Junot not only pocketed all the money he pretended was due to his aide-de-camp, but the whole sum contained in the bank, which was double that amount. It was believed by everyone present that this was an affair arranged between him and his aide-de-camp beforehand to pillage the bank. What a commander, what a general, and what an ambassador!

Fitte, the secretary of our embassy to Portugal, was formerly an abbé, and must be well remembered in your country, where he passed some years as an emigrant, but was, in fact, a spy of Talleyrand. I am told that, by his intrigues, he even succeeded in swindling your ministers out of a sum of money by some plausible schemes he proposed to them. He is, as well as all other apostate priests, a very dangerous man, and an immoral and unprincipled wretch. During the time of Robespierre he is said to have caused the murder of his elder brother and younger sister; the former he denounced to appropriate to himself his wealth, and the latter he accused of fanaticism because she refused to cohabit with him. He daily boasts of the great protection and great friendship of Talleyrand. *Qualis rex, talis grex.*

LETTER LIX

Paris, *September*, 1805.

My Lord,—In some of the ancient republics, all citizens who, in time of danger and trouble, remained *neutral*, were punished as traitors or treated as enemies. When, by our Revolution, civilized society and the European commonwealth were menaced with a total overthrow, had each member of it been considered in the same light, and subjected to the same laws, some individual states might, perhaps, have been less wealthy, but the whole community would have been more happy and more tranquil, which would have been much better. It was a great error in the powerful league of 1793 to admit any neutrality at all: every Government that did not combat rebellion should have been considered and treated as its ally. The man who continues *neutral*, though only a passenger, when hands are wanted to preserve the vessel from sinking, deserves to be thrown overboard, to be swallowed up by the waves and to perish the first. Had all other nations been united and unanimous, during 1793 and 1794, against the monster, Jacobinism, we should not have heard of either Jacobin directors, Jacobin consuls, or a Jacobin Emperor. But then, from a petty regard to a temporary profit, they entered into a truce with a revolutionary volcano, which, sooner or later, will consume them all; for I am afraid that it is now too late for all human power, with all human means, to preserve any state, any government, or any people, from suffering by the threatening conflagration. Switzerland, Venice, Geneva, Genoa and Tuscany have already gathered the poisoned fruits of their neutrality. Let but Bonaparte establish himself undisturbed in Hanover some years longer, and you will see the neutral Hanse Towns, neutral Prussia and neutral Denmark visited with all the evils of invasion, pillage and destruction, and the independence of the nations in the North will be buried in the rubbish of the liberties of the people of the South of Europe.

These ideas have frequently occurred to me, on hearing *our* agents pronounce, and *their* dupes repeat: "Oh! the wise Government of Denmark! Oh, what a wise statesman the Danish minister, Count Bernstorf!" I do not deny that the late Count Bernstorf was a great politician; but I assert also, that his was a greatness more calculated for regular times than for periods of unusual political convulsion. Like your Pitt, the Russian Woronzow, and the Austrian Colloredo, he was too honest to judge soundly and to act rightly, according to the present situation of affairs. He adhered too much to the old routine, and did not perceive the immense difference between the government of a revolutionary ruler and the government of a Louis XIII. or a Louis XIV. I am certain, had he still been alive, he would have repented of his errors, and tried to have repaired them.

His son, the present Danish Minister, follows his father's plans, and adheres, in 1805, to a system laid down by him in 1795; while the alterations that have occurred within these ten years have more affected the real and relative power and weakness of states than all the revolutions which have been produced by the insurrections, wars and pacifications of the two preceding centuries. He has even gone farther, in some parts of his administration, than his father ever intended. Without remembering the political TRUTH, that a weak state which courts the alliance of a powerful neighbour always becomes a vassal, while desiring to become an ally, he has attempted to exchange the connections of Denmark and Russia for new ones with Prussia; and forgotten the obligations of the Cabinet of Copenhagen to the Cabinet of St. Petersburg, and the interested policy of the House of Brandenburg. That, on the contrary, Russia has always been a generous ally of Denmark, the flourishing state of the Danish dominions since the beginning of the last century evinces. Its distance and geographical position prevent all encroachments from being feared or attempted ; while at the same time it affords protection equally against the rivalry of Sweden and ambition of Prussia.

The Prince Royal of Denmark is patriotic as well as enlightened, and would rule with more true policy and lustre were he to follow seldomer the advice of his counsellors and oftener the dictates of his own mind. Count de Schimmelmann, Count de Reventlow, and Count Bernstorf, are all good and moral characters ; but I fear that their united capacity taken together will not fill up the vacancy left in the Danish Cabinet by the death of its late prime minister. I have been personally acquainted with them all three, but I draw my conclusions from the acts of their administration, not from my own knowledge. Had the late Count Bernstorf held the ministerial helm in 1803, a paragraph in the *Moniteur* would never have disbanded a Danish army in Holstein ; nor would, in 1805, intriguers have been endured who preached neutrality, after witnessing repeated violation of the law of nations, not on the remote banks of the Rhine, but on the Danish frontiers, on the Danish territory, on the banks of the Elbe.

It certainly was no compliment to His Danish Majesty when our Government sent Grouvelle as a representative to Copenhagen, a man who owed his education and information to the Condé branch of the Bourbons, and who afterwards audaciously and sacrilegiously read the sentence of death on the chief of that family, on his good and legitimate King, Louis XVI. It can neither be called dignity nor prudence in the Cabinet of Denmark to suffer this regicide to serve as a point of rally to sedition and innovation; to be the official propagator of revolutionary doctrines, and an official protector of all proselytes and sectaries of this anti-social faith.

Before the Revolution a secretary to the Prince of Condé, Grouvelle was trusted and rewarded by His Serene Highness, and in return betrayed his confidence, and repaid benefactions and generosity with calumny and persecution, when his patron was obliged to seek safety in emigration against the assassins of successful rebellion. When the national seals were put on the estates of the Prince, he appropriated to himself not only the whole of His Highness's library, but a part of his plate. Even the wardrobe and the cellar were laid under contributions by this domestic marauder.

With natural genius and acquired experience, Grouvelle unites impudence and immorality; and those on whom he fixes for his prey are therefore easily duped, and irremediably undone. He has furnished disciples to all factions and to all sects, assassins to the revolutionary tribunals, as well as victims for the revolutionary guillotine; sans-culottes to Robespierre, Septembrizers to Marat, *republicans* to the Directory, spies to Talleyrand, and slaves to Bonaparte, who, in 1800, nominated him a tribune, but in 1804 disgraced him, because he wished that the Duke of Enghien had rather been secretly poisoned in Baden, than publicly condemned and privately executed in France.

Our present minister at the Court of Copenhagen, d'Aguesseau, has no virtues to boast of, but also no crimes to blush for. With inferior capacity, he is only considered by Talleyrand as an inferior intriguer, employed in a country ruled by an inferior policy, neither feared nor esteemed by our Government. His secretary, Desaugiers the elder, is our real and confidential firebrand in the North, commissioned to keep burning those materials of combustion which Grouvelle and others of our incendiaries have lighted and illuminated in Holstein, Denmark, Sweden and Norway.

LETTER LX.

Paris, *October*, 1805.

My Lord,—The insatiable avarice of all the members of the Bonaparte family has already and frequently been mentioned; some of our *philosophers*, however, pretend that ambition and vanity exclude from the mind of Napoleon Bonaparte the passion of covetousness; that he pillages only to get money to pay his military plunderers, and hoards treasures only to purchase slaves, or to recompense the associates and instruments of his authority.

Whether their assertions be just or not, I will not take upon myself to decide; but to judge from the great number of imperial and royal palaces, from the great augmentation of the imperial and royal domains; from the immense and valuable quantity of diamonds, jewels, pictures, statues, libraries, museums, &c., disinterestedness and self-denial are certainly not among Napoleon's virtues.

In France, he not only disposes of all the former palaces and extensive demesnes of our King, but has greatly increased them, by national property and by lands and estates bought by the imperial treasury, or confiscated by imperial decrees. In Italy, he has, by an official act, declared to be the property of his crown, first, the royal palace at Milan, and a royal villa, which he now calls Villa Bonaparte; second, the palace of Monza and its dependencies; third, the palace of Mantua, the palace of Thé, and the *ci-devant* ducal palace of Modena; fourth, a palace situated in the vicinity of Brescia, and another palace in the vicinity of Bologna; fifth, the *ci-devant* ducal palaces of Parma and Placenza; sixth, the beautiful forest of Tesin. Ten millions were, besides, ordered to be drawn out of the royal treasury at Milan to purchase lands for the formation of a park, pleasure-grounds, &c.

To these are added all the royal palaces and domains of the former Kings of Sardinia, of the Dukes of Brabant, of the Counts of Flanders, of the German Electors, princes, dukes, counts, barons, &c., who, before the last war, were Sovereigns on the right bank of the Rhine. I have seen a list, according to which the number of palaces and châteaux appertaining to Napoleon as Emperor and King, are stated to be seventy-nine; so that he may change his habitations six times in the month, without occupying during the same year the same palace, and, nevertheless, always *sleep* at home.

In this number are not included the *private* châteaux and estates of the Empress, or those of the Princes and Princesses Bonaparte. Madame Napoleon has purchased, since her husband's Consulate, in her own name, or in the name of her children, nine estates with their châteaux, four national forests, and six hotels at Paris. Joseph Bonaparte possesses four estates and châteaux in France, three hotels at Paris and at Brussels, three châteaux and estates in Italy, and one hotel at Milan, and another at Turin. Lucien Bonaparte has now remaining only one hotel at Paris, another at Bonne, and a third at Chambéry. He has one estate in Burgundy, two in Languedoc, and one in the vicinity of this capital. At Bologna, Ferrara, Florence and Rome, he has his own hotels, and in the Papal States he has obtained, in exchange for property in France, three châteaux with their dependencies. Louis Bonaparte has three hotels at Paris, one at Cologne, one at Strasburg, and one at Lyons. He has two estates in Flanders, three in Burgundy, one in Franche-Comté, and another in Alsace. He has also a château four leagues from this city. At Genoa he has a beautiful hotel, and upon the Genoese territory a large estate. He has bought three plantations at Martinico, and two at Guadeloupe. To Jerome Bonaparte has hitherto been presented only an estate in Brabant, and a hotel in this capital. Some of the former domains of the House of Orange, in the Batavian Republic, have been purchased by the agents of our Government, and are said to be intended for him.

But while Napoleon Bonaparte has thus heaped wealth on his wife and his brothers, his mother and sisters have not been neglected or left unprovided for. Madame Bonaparte, his mother, has one hotel at Paris, one at Turin, one at Milan, and one at Rome. Her estates in France are four, and in Italy two. Madame Bacciochi, Princess of Piombino and Lucca, possesses two hotels in this capital, and one palace at Piombino and another at Lucca. Of her estates in France, she has only retained two, but she has three in the kingdom of Italy, and four in her husband's and her own dominions. The Princess Santa Cruce possesses one hotel at Rome and four châteaux in the Papal territory. At Milan she has, as well as at Turin and at Paris, hotels given her by her imperial brother, together with two estates in France, one in Piedmont, and two in Lombardy. The Princess Murat is mistress of two hotels here, one at Brussels, one at Tours, and one at Bordeaux, together with three estates on this, and five on the other side of the Alps. The Princess Borghese has purchased three plantations at Guadeloupe, and two at Martinico, with a part of the treasures left her by her first husband, Le Clerc. With her present husband she received two palaces at Rome, and three estates on the Roman territory; and her imperial brother has presented her with one hotel at Paris, one at Cologne, one at Turin, and one at Genoa, together with three estates in France and five in Italy. For his mother, and for each of his sisters, Napoleon has also purchased estates, or lands to form estates, in their native island of Corsica.

The other near or distant relatives of the Emperor and King have also experienced his bounty. Cardinal Fesch has his hotels at Paris, Milan, Lyons, Turin and Rome; with estates both in France and Italy. Seventeen, either first, second, or third cousins, by his father's or mother's side, have all obtained estates either in the French empire, or in the kingdom of Italy, as well as all brothers, sisters, or cousins of his own wife, and the wives of his brothers, or of the husbands of his sisters. Their exact number cannot well be known, but a gentleman who has long been collecting materials for some future history of the House of Bonaparte, and of the French empire, has already shown me sixty-six names of individuals of that description, and of both sexes, who all, thanks to the imperial liberality, have suddenly and unexpectedly become people of property.

When you consider that all these immense riches have been seized and distributed within the short period of five years, it is not hazardous to say that, in the annals of Europe, another such revolution in property, as well as in power, is not to be found. The wealth of the families of all other Sovereigns taken together does not amount to half the value of what the Bonapartes have acquired and possess.

Your country, more than any other upon earth, has to be alarmed at this revolution of property. Richer than any other nation, you have more to apprehend ; besides, it threatens you more, both as our frequent enemies and as our national rivals ; as a barrier against our plans of universal dominion, and as our superiors in pecuniary resources. May we never live to see the day when the mandates of Bonaparte or Talleyrand are honoured at London, as at Amsterdam, Madrid, Milan and Rome. The misery of ages to come will then be certain, and posterity will regard as comparative happiness, the sufferings of their forefathers. It is not probable that those who have so successfully pillaged all surrounding states will rest contented until you are involved in the same ruin. Union among yourselves only can preserve you from perishing in the universal wreck ; by this you will at least gain time, and may hope to profit by probable changes and unexpected accidents.

LETTER LXI

PARIS, *October*, 1805.

MY LORD,—The counsellor of state and intendant of the imperial civil list, Daru, paid for the place of a commissary-general of our army in Germany the immense sum of six millions of livres—£250,000—which was divided between Madame Bonaparte (the mother), Madame Napoleon Bonaparte, Princess Louis Bonaparte, Princess Murat and the Princess of Borghese. By this you may conclude in what manner we intend to treat the wretched inhabitants of the other side of the Rhine. This Daru is too good a calculator and too fond of money to throw away his expenses; he is master of a great fortune, made entirely by his arithmetical talents, which have enabled him for years to break all the principal gambling-banks on the Continent, where he has travelled for no other purpose. On his return here, he became the terror of all our gamesters, who offered him an annuity of one hundred thousand livres—£4,000—not to play; but as this sum would have been deducted from what is weekly paid to Fouché, this minister sent him an order not to approach a gambling-table, under pain of being transported to Cayenne. He obeyed, but the bankers soon experienced that he had deputies, and for fear that even from the other side of the Atlantic he might forward his calculations hither, Fouché recommended him, for a *small* douceur, to the office of an intendant of Bonaparte's civil list, upon condition of never, directly or indirectly, injuring our gambling-banks. He has kept his promise with regard to France, but made, last spring, a gambling tour in Italy and Germany, which, he avows, produced him nine millions of livres—£375,000. He always points, but never keeps a bank. He begins to be so well known in many parts of the Continent, that the instant he arrives all banks are shut up, and remain so until his departure. This was the case at Florence last April. He travels always in style, accompanied by two mistresses and four servants. He is a chevalier of the Legion of Honour.

He will, however, have some difficulty to make a great profit by his calculations in Germany, as many of the generals are better acquainted than he with the country, where their extortions and dilapidations have been felt and lamented for these ten years past. Augereau, Bernadotte, Ney, Van Damme, and other of our military banditti, have long been the terror of the Germans and the reproach of France.

In a former letter I have introduced to you our field-marshal, Bernadotte, of whom Augereau may justly be called an elder revolutionary brother—like him, a Parisian by birth, and, like him, serving as a common soldier before the Revolution. But he has this *merit* above Bernadotte, that he began his political career as a police spy, and finished his first military engagement by desertion into foreign countries, in most of which, after again enlisting and again deserting, he was also again taken and again flogged. Italy has, indeed, since he has been made a general, been more the scene of his devastations than Germany. Lombardy and Venice will not soon forget the thousands he butchered, and the millions he plundered; that with hands reeking with blood, and stained with human gore, he seized the trinkets which devotion had given to sanctity, to ornament the fingers of an assassin, or decorate the bosom of a harlot. The outrages he committed during 1796 and 1797, in Italy, are too numerous to find place in any letter, even were they not disgusting to relate, and too enormous and too improbable to be believed. He frequently transformed the temples of the divinity into brothels for prostitution; and virgins who had consecrated themselves to remain the unpolluted servants of a God, he bayoneted into dens of impurity, infamy and profligacy; and in these abominations he prided himself. In August,

1797, on his way to Paris to take command of the sbirri, who on the 4th of the following September hunted away or imprisoned the representatives of the people of the Legislative Body, he paid a prostitute, with whom he had passed the night at Pavia, with a draft for fifty louis d'or on the municipality of that town, who dared not dishonour it; but they kept the draft, and in 1799, handed it over to General Melas, who sent it to Vienna, where I saw the very original.

The general and grand officer of Bonaparte's Legion of Honour, Van Damme, is another of our military heroes of the same stamp. A barber, and son of a Flemish barber, he enlisted as a soldier, robbed, and was condemned to be hanged. The humanity of the judge preserved him from the gallows; but he was burnt on the shoulders, flogged by the public executioner, and doomed to serve as a galley-slave for life. The Revolution broke his fetters, made him a Jacobin, a patriot and a general; but the first use he made of his good fortune was to cause the judge, his benefactor, to be guillotined, and to appropriate to himself the estate of the family. He was cashiered by Pichegru, and dishonoured by Moreau, for his ferocity and plunder in Holland and Germany; but Bonaparte restored him to rank and confidence; and by a douceur of twelve hundred thousand livres — £50,000 —

properly applied and divided between some of the members of the Bonaparte family, he procured the place of a governor at Lille, and a commander-in-chief of the *ci-devant* Flanders. In landed property, in jewels, in amount in the funds, and in ready-money (he always keeps, from prudence, six hundred thousand livres—£25,000—in gold), his riches amount to eight millions of livres—£335,000. For a *ci-devant sans-culotte* barber and galley-slave, you must grant this is a very *modest* sum.

LETTER LXII

PARIS, *October*, 1805.

MY LORD,—You must often have been surprised at the immense wealth which, from the best and often authentic information, I have informed you our generals and public functionaries have extorted and possess ; but the catalogue of private rapine committed, without authority, by our soldiers, officers, commissaries and generals, is likewise immense, and surpassing often the exactions of a *legal* kind—that is to say, those authorized by our Government itself, or by its civil and military representatives. It comprehends the innumerable requisitions demanded and enforced, whether as loans, or in provisions or merchandise, or in money as an equivalent for both ; the levies of men, of horses, oxen and carriages ; *corvées* of all kinds ; the emptying of magazines for the service of our armies ; in short, whatever was required for the maintenance, a portion of the pay, and divers wants of those armies, from the time they had posted themselves in Brabant, Holland, Italy, Switzerland, and on either bank of the Rhine. Add to this the pillage of public or private warehouses, granaries and magazines, whether belonging to individuals, to the state, to societies, to towns, to hospitals, and even to orphan-houses.

But these and other sorts of *requisitions*, under the appellation of subsistence necessary for the armies, and for what was wanted for accoutring, quartering, or removing them, included also an infinite consumption for the pleasures, luxuries, whims and debaucheries of our civil or military commanders. Most of those articles were delivered in kind, and what were not used were set up to auction, converted into ready-money, and divided among the plunderers.

In 1797, General Ney had the command in the vicinity of the free and imperial city of Wetzlar. He there put in requisition all private stores of cloths; and after disposing of them by a public sale, retook them upon another requisition from the purchasers, and sold them a second time. Leather and linen underwent the same operation. Volumes might be filled with similar examples, all of public notoriety.

This General Ney, who is now one of the principal commanders under Bonaparte in Germany, was a bankrupt tobacconist at Strasburg in 1790, and is the son of an old-clothes man of *Sarre Louis*, where he was born in 1765. Having entered as a common soldier in the regiment of Alsace, to escape the pursuit of his creditors, he was there picked up by some Jacobin emissaries, whom he assisted to seduce the men into an insurrection, which obliged most of the officers to emigrate. From that period he began to distinguish himself as an orator of the Jacobin clubs, and was therefore, by his associates, promoted by one step to an adjutant-general. Brave and enterprising, ambitious for advancement, and greedy after riches, he seized every opportunity to distinguish and enrich himself; and as fortune supported his endeavours, he was in a short time made a general of division, and acquired a property of several millions. This is his first campaign under Bonaparte, having previously served only under Pichegru, Moreau and Le Courbe.

He, with General Richepanse, was one of the first generals supposed to be attached to their former chief, General Moreau, whom Bonaparte seduced into his interest. In the autumn of 1802, when the Helvetic Republic attempted to recover their lost independence, Ney was appointed commander-in-chief of the French army in Switzerland, and ambassador from the First Consul to the Helvetic Government. He there conducted himself so much to the satisfaction of Bonaparte, that on the rupture with your country, he was made commander of the camp near Montreuil; and last year his wife was received as a maid-of-honour to the Empress of the French.

This maid-of-honour is the daughter of a washerwoman, and was kept by a man-milliner at Strasburg at the time that she eloped with Ney. With him she had made four campaigns as a mistress before the municipality of Coblentz made her his wife. Her conduct since has corresponded with that of her husband. When he publicly lived with mistresses, she did not live privately with her gallants, but the instant the Emperor of the French told him to save appearances, if he desired a place for his wife at the Imperial Court, he showed himself the most attentive and faithful of husbands, and she the most tender and dutiful of wives. Her manners are not polished, but they are pleasing; and though not handsome in her person, she is lively; and her conversation is entertaining, and her society agreeable. The Princess Louis Bonaparte is particularly fond of her, more so than Napoleon perhaps desires. She has a fault common with most of our Court ladies; she cannot resist, when opportunity presents itself, the temptation of gambling, and she is far from being fortunate. Report says that more than once she has been reduced to acquit her gambling debts by personal favours.

Another of our generals, and the richest of them all who are now serving under Bonaparte, is his brother-in-law, *Prince* Murat. According to some, he had been a Septembrizer, terrorist, Jacobin, robber and assassin long before he obtained his first commission as an officer, which was given him by the recommendation of Marat, whom he in return afterwards wished to *immortalize*, by the exchange of one letter in his own name, and by calling himself M*a*rat instead of M*u*rat. Others, however, declare that his father was an honest cobbler, very superstitious, residing at Bastide, near Cahors, and destined his son to be a capuchin friar, and that he was in his novitiate when the Revolution tempted him to exchange the frock of the monk for the regimentals of a soldier. In what manner, or by what achievements, he gained promotion is not certain, but in 1796 he was a chief of brigade, and an aide-de-camp of Bonaparte, with whom he went to Egypt, and returned thence with him, and who, in 1801, married him to his sister, Maria Annunciade, in 1803 made him a Governor of Paris, and in 1804 a Prince!

The wealth which Murat has collected, during his military service, and by his matrimonial campaign, is rated at upwards of fifty millions of livres—£2,100,000. The landed property he possesses in France alone has cost him forty-two millions—£1,750,000—and it is whispered that the estates bought in the name of his wife, both in France and Italy, are not worth much less. A brother-in-law of his, who was a smith, he has made a legislator; and an uncle, who was a tailor, he has placed in the senate. A cousin of his, who was a chimney-sweeper, is now a tribune; and his niece, who was an apprentice to a mantua-maker, is now married to one of the Emperor's chamberlains. He has been very generous to all his relations, and would not have been ashamed, even, to present his parents at the Imperial Court, had not the mother, on the first information of his princely rank, lost her life, and the father his senses, from surprise and joy. The millions are not few that he has procured his relatives an opportunity to gain. His brother-in-law, the legislator, is worth three millions of livres—£125,000.

It has been asserted before, and I repeat it again: "It is avarice, and not the mania of innovation, or the jargon of liberty, that has led, and ever will lead, the Revolution—its promoters, its accomplices and its instruments. Wherever they penetrate, plunder follows; rapine was their first object, of which ferocity has been but the means. The French Revolution was fostered by robbery and murder; two nurses that will adhere to her to the last hour of her existence."

General Murat is the trusty executioner of all the Emperor's secret deeds of vengeance, or public acts of revolutionary justice. It was under his private responsibility that Pichegru, Moreau and Georges were guarded: and he saw Pichegru strangled, Georges guillotined, and Moreau on his way to his place of exile. After the seizure and trial of the Duke of Enghien, some doubts existed with Napoleon whether even the soldiers of his Italian guard would fire at this Prince. "If they hesitate," said Murat, who commanded the *expedition* in the wood of Vincennes, "my pistols are loaded, and I will blow out his brains."

His wife is the greatest coquette of the Bonaparte family. Murat was, at first, after his marriage, rather jealous of his brother-in-law, Lucien, whom he even fought; but Napoleon having assured him, upon his word of honour, that his suspicions were unfounded, he is now the model of complaisant and indulgent husbands; but his mistresses are *nearly* as numerous as Madame Murat's favourites. He has a young aide-de-camp of the name of Flahault, a son of Talleyrand, while bishop of Autun, by the then Countess de Flahault, whom Madame Murat would not have been sorry to have had for a consoler at Paris, while her princely spouse was desolating Germany.

LETTER LXIII

PARIS, *October*, 1805.

MY LORD,—Since Bonaparte's departure for Germany, the vigilance of the police has much increased: our patrols are doubled during the night, and our spies more numerous and more insolent during the day. Many *suspected* persons have also been exiled to some distance from this capital, while others, for a *measure of safety*, have been shut up in the Temple, or in the Castle of Vincennes. These *lettres de cachet*, or mandates of arrest, are expedited during the Emperor's absence exclusively by his brother Louis, after a report, or upon a request, of the minister of police, Fouché.

I have mentioned to you before that Louis Bonaparte is both a drunkard and a libertine. When a young and unprincipled man of such propensities enjoys an unrestrained authority, it cannot be surprising to hear that he has abused it. He had not been his brother's military viceroy for twenty-four hours before one set of our Parisians were amused, while others were shocked and scandalized, at a tragical intrigue enterprized by His Imperial Highness.

Happening to see at the opera a very handsome young woman in the boxes, he despatched one of his aides-de-camp to reconnoitre the ground, and to find out who she was. All *gentlemen* attached to his person or household are also his pimps, and are no novices in forming or executing plans of seduction. Caulincourt (the officer he employed in this affair) returned soon, but had succeeded only in one part of the business. He had not been able to speak to the lady, but was informed that she had only been married a fortnight to a manufacturer of Lyons, who was seated by her side, jealous of his wife as a lover of his mistress. He gave at the same time as his opinion that it would be necessary to employ the police commissary to arrest the husband when he left the play, under some pretext or other, while some of the *friends* of Prince Louis took advantage of the confusion to seize the wife, and carry her to his hotel. An order was directly signed by Louis, according to which the police commissary, Chazot, was to arrest the manufacturer Leboure, of Lyons, and put him into a post-chaise, under the care of two gendarmes, who were to see him safe to Lyons, where he was to sign a promise of not returning to Paris without the permission of Government, being suspected of stock-jobbing (*agiotage*).

Everything succeeded according to the proposal of Caulincourt, and Louis found Madame Leboure crying in his saloon. It is said that she promised to surrender her virtue upon condition of only once more seeing her husband, to be certain that he was not murdered, but that Louis refused, and obtained by brutal force, and the assistance of his infamous associates, that conquest over her honour, which had not been yielded to his entreaties or threats. His enjoyment, however, was but of short continuance; he had no sooner fallen asleep than his poor injured victim left the bed, and, flying into his ante-room, stabbed herself with his sword. On the next morning she was found a corpse, weltering in her blood. In the hope of burying this infamy in secrecy, her corpse was, on the next evening, when it was dark, put into a sack, and thrown into the river, where, being afterwards discovered, the police agents gave out that she had fallen the victim of assassins. But when Madame Leboure was thus seized at the opera, besides her husband, her parents and a brother were in her company, and the latter did not lose sight of the carriage in which his sister was placed till it had entered the hotel of Louis Bonaparte, where, on the next day, he, with his father, in vain claimed her. As soon as the husband was informed of the untimely end of his wife, he wrote a letter to her murderer, and shot himself immediately afterwards through the head, but his own head was not the place where he should have sent the bullet; to destroy with it the cause of his wretchedness would only have been an act of retaliation, in a country where power forces the law to lie dormant, and where justice is invoked in vain when the criminal is powerful.

I have said that this intrigue, as it is styled by courtesy in our fashionable circles, *amused* one part of the Parisians; and I believe the word *amuse* is not improperly employed in this instance. At a dozen parties where I have been since, this unfortunate adventure has always been an object of conversation, of *witticisms*, but not of blame, except at Madame Fouché's, where Madame Leboure was very much blamed indeed *for having been so over nice*, and *foolishly scrupulous*.

Another intrigue of His Imperial Highness, which did not, indeed, end tragically, was related last night, at the tea-party of Madame Récamier. A man of the name of Deroux had lately been condemned by our criminal tribunal, for forging bills of exchange, to stand in the pillory six hours, and after being marked with a hot iron on his shoulders, to work in the galleys for twenty years. His daughter, a young girl, under fifteen, who lived with her grandmother (having lost her mother), went, accompanied by the old lady, and presented a petition to Louis, in favour of her father. Her youth and modesty, more than her beauty, inspired the unprincipled libertine with a desire of ruining innocence, under the colour of clemency to guilt. He ordered her to call on his chamberlain, Darinsson, in an hour, and she should obtain an answer. There, either seduced by paternal affection, intimidated by threats, or imposed upon by delusive and engaging promises, she exchanged her virtue for an order of release for her parent; and so satisfied was Louis with his bargain, that he added her to the number of his regular mistresses.

As soon as Deroux had recovered his liberty, he visited his daughter in her new situation, where he saw an order of Louis, on the imperial treasury, for twelve thousand livres—£500—destined to pay the upholsterer who had furnished her apartment. This gave him, no doubt, the idea of making the Prince pay a higher value for his child, and he forged another order for sixty thousand livres — £2,500 — so closely resembling it that it was without suspicion acquitted by the imperial treasurer. Possessing this money, he fabricated a pass, in the name of Louis, as a courier carrying despatches to the Emperor in Germany, with which he set out, and arrived safe on the other side of the Rhine. His forgeries were only discovered after he had written a letter from Frankfort to Louis, acquitting his daughter of all knowledge of what he had done. In the first moment of anger, her imperial lover ordered her to be arrested, but he has since forgiven her, and taken her back to his favour. This *trick* of Deroux has pleased Fouché, who long opposed his release, from a knowledge of his dangerous talent and vicious character. He had once before released himself with a forged order from the minister of police, whose handwriting he had only seen for a minute upon his own mandate of imprisonment.

LETTER LXIV

PARIS, *October*, 1805.

MY LORD,—Though loudly complained of by the Cabinet of St. Cloud, the Cabinet of St. Petersburg has conducted itself in these critical times with prudence without weakness, and with firmness without obstinacy. In its connections with our Government it has never lost sight of its own dignity, and, therefore, never endured without resentment those impertinent innovations in the etiquette of our Court, and in the manner and language of our Emperor to the representatives of legitimate sovereigns. Had similar becoming sentiments directed the councils of all other princes and the behaviour of their ambassadors here, spirited remonstrances might have moderated the pretensions or passions of upstart vanity, while a forbearance and silence, equally impolitic and shameful, have augmented insolence by flattering the pride of an insupportable and outrageous ambition.

The Emperor of Russia would not have been so well represented here, had he not been so wisely served and advised in his council chamber at St. Petersburg. Ignorance and folly commonly select fools for their agents, while genius and capacity employ men of their own mould, and of their own cast. It is a remarkable truth that, notwithstanding the frequent revolutions in Russia, since the death of Peter the First the ministerial helm has always been in able hands; the progressive and uninterrupted increase of the real and relative power of the Russian empire evinces the reality of this assertion.

The Russian chancellor, Count Alexander Woronzoff, may be justly called the chief of political veterans, whether his talents or long services are considered. Catherine II., though a voluptuous Princess, was a great Sovereign, and a competent judge of merit; and it was her unbiased choice that seated Count Woronzoff, while yet young, in her councils. Though the intrigues of favourites have sometimes removed him, he always retired with the esteem of his Sovereign, and was recalled without caballing or cringing to return. He is admired, by all who have the honour of approaching him, as much for his obliging condescension as for his great information. No petty views, no petty caprices, no petty vengeances find room in his generous bosom. He is known to have conferred benefactions, not only on his enemies, but on those who, at the very time, were meditating his destruction. His opinion is that a patriotic minister should regard no others as his enemies but those conspiring against their country, and acknowledge no friends or favourites incapable of well serving the State. Prince de Z—— waited on him one day, and, after hesitating some time, began to compliment him on his liberal sentiments, and concluded by asking the place of a governor for his cousin, with whom he had reason to suppose the Count much offended. "I am happy," said his Excellency, "to oblige you, and to do my duty at the same time. Here is a libel he wrote against me, and presented to the Empress, who graciously has communicated it to me, in answer to my recommendation of him yesterday to the place you ask for him to-day. Read what I have written on the libel, and you will be convinced that it will not be my fault if he is not to-day a governor." In two hours afterwards, the nomination was announced to Prince de Z——, who was himself at the head of a cabal against the minister. In any country such an act would have been laudable, but where despotism rules with unopposed sway, it is both honourable and praiseworthy.

Prince Adam de Czartorinsky, the assistant of Count de Woronzoff, and minister of the foreign department, unites, with the vigour of youth, the experience of age. He has travelled in most countries of Europe, not solely to figure at Courts, to dance at balls, to look at pictures, or to collect curiosities, but to study the characters of the people, the laws by which they are governed, and their moral or social influence with regard to their comforts or misery. He, therefore, brought back with him a stock of knowledge not to be acquired from books, but only found in the world by frequenting different and opposite societies with observation, penetration and genius. With manners as polished as his mind is well informed, he not only possesses the favour, but the friendship of his Prince; and, what is still more rare, is worthy of both. All sovereigns have favourites, few ever had any friends; because it is more easy to flatter vanity than to display a liberal disinterestedness; to bow meanly than to instruct or to guide with delicacy and dignity; to abuse the confidence of the Prince than to use it to his honour, and to the advantage of his government.

That such a monarch as an Alexander, and such ministers as Count de Woronzoff and Prince de Czartorinsky, should appoint a Count de Markoff to a high and important post was not unexpected by anyone not ignorant of his merit.

Count de Markoff was, early in the reign of Catherine II., employed in the office of the foreign department at St. Petersburg, and was, whilst young, entrusted with several important negotiations at the Courts of Berlin and Vienna, when Prussia had proposed the first partition of Poland. He afterwards went on his travels, from which he was recalled to fill the place of an ambassador to the late King of Sweden, Gustavus III. He was succeeded, in 1784, at Stockholm, by Count Muschin Puschin, after being appointed a secretary of state in his own country, a post he occupied with distinction, until the death of Catherine II., when Paul the First revenged upon him, as well as on most others of the faithful servants of this Princess, his discontent with his mother. He was then exiled to his estates, where he retired with the esteem of all those who had known him. In 1801, immediately after his accession to the throne, Alexander invited Count de Markoff to his Court and council, and the trusty but difficult task of representing a legitimate Sovereign at the Court of our upstart usurper was conferred on him. I imagine that I see the great surprise of this nobleman, when, for the first time, he entered the audience-chamber of our little great man, and saw him fretting, staring, swearing, abusing to right and to left, for one smile conferring twenty frowns, and for one civil word making use of fifty harsh expressions, marching in the diplomatic audience as at the head of his troops, and commanding foreign ambassadors as his French soldiers. I have heard that the report of Count de Markoff to his Court, describing this new and rare show, is a *chef-d'œuvre* of wit, equally amusing and instructive. He is said to have requested of his Cabinet new and particular orders how to act—whether as the representative of an independent Sovereign, or, as most of the other members of the foreign diplomatic corps in France, like a valet of the First Consul; and that, in the latter case, he implored as a favour an immediate recall; preferring, had he no other choice left, sooner to work in the mines at Siberia than to wear in France the disgraceful fetters of a Bonaparte. His subsequent dignified conduct proves the answer of his Court.

Talleyrand's craft and dissimulation could not delude the sagacity of Count de Markoff, who was, therefore, soon less liked by the minister than by the First Consul. All kind of low, vulgar and revolutionary chicanery was made use of to vex or to provoke the Russian ambassador. Sometimes he was reproached with having emigrants in his service; another time protection was refused to one of his secretaries, under pretence that he was a Sardinian subject. Russian travellers were insulted, and detained on the most frivolous pretences. Two Russian noblemen were even arrested on our side of the Rhine, because Talleyrand had *forgotten* to sign his name to their passes, which were otherwise in order. The fact was that our minister suspected them of carrying some papers which he wanted to see, and, therefore, wrote his name with an ink of such a composition that, after a certain number of days, everything written with it disappeared. Their effects and papers were strictly searched by an agent preceding them from this capital, but nothing was found, our minister being misinformed by his spies.

When Count de Markoff left Sweden, he carried with him an actress of the French theatre at Stockholm, Madame Hus, an Alsatian by birth, but who had quitted her country twelve years before the Revolution, and could, therefore, never be included among emigrants. She had continued as a mistress with this nobleman, is the mother of several children by him, and an agreeable companion to him, who has never been married. As I have often said, Talleyrand is much obliged to any foreign diplomatic agent who allows him to be the indirect provider or procurer of his mistresses. After in vain tempting Count de Markoff with new objects, he introduced to the acquaintance of Madame Hus some of his female emissaries. Their manœuvres, their insinuations, and even their presents were all thrown away. The lady remained the faithful friend, and therefore refused with indignation to degrade herself into a spy on her lover. Our minister then first discovered that, not only was Madame Hus an emigrant, but had been a great benefactress and constant companion of emigrants at St. Petersburg, and of course deserved to be watched, if not punished. Count de Markoff is reported to have said to Talleyrand on this grave subject, in the presence of two other foreign ambassadors: "Apropos! what shall I do to prevent my poor Madame Hus from being shot as an emigrant, and my poor children from becoming prematurely orphans?"— "Sir," said our diplomatic oracle, "she should have petitioned the First Consul for a permission to return to France before she entered it; but out of regard for you, if she is *prudent*, she will not, I daresay, be troubled by our Government."—"I should be sorry if she was not," replied the Count with a significant look; and here this grand affair ended, to the great entertainment of those foreign agents who dared to smile or to laugh.

LETTER LXV

PARIS, *October*, 1805.

MY LORD,—The Legion of Honour, though only proclaimed upon Bonaparte's assumption of the imperial rank, dates from the first year of his consulate. To prepare the public mind for a progressive elevation of himself, and for consequential distinctions among all classes of his subjects, he distributed among the military, arms of honour, to which were attached precedence and privileges granted by him, and, therefore, liable to cease with his power or life. The number of these arms increased in proportion to the approach of the period fixed for the change of his title and the erection of his throne. When he judged them numerous enough to support his changes, he made all these wearers of arms of honour knights. Never before were so many chevaliers created *en masse:* they amounted to no less than twenty-two thousand four hundred, distributed in the different corps of different armies, but principally in the army of England. To these were afterwards joined five thousand nine hundred civil functionaries, men of letters, artists, &c. To remove, however, all ideas of equality, even among the members of the Legion of Honour, they were divided into four classes—grand officers, commanders, officers and simple *legionaries*.

Everyone who has observed Bonaparte's incessant endeavours to intrude himself among the Sovereigns of Europe, was convinced that he would cajole, or force, as many of them as he could into his revolutionary knighthood; but I heard men, who are not ignorant of the selfishness and corruption of our times, deny the possibility of any independent Prince suffering his name to be registered among criminals of every description, from the thief who picked the pockets of his fellow-citizens in the street, down to the regicide who sat in judgment and condemned his King; from the plunderers who have laid waste provinces, republics and kingdoms, down to the assassins who shot, drowned or guillotined their countrymen *en masse*. For my part, I never had but one opinion, and unfortunately it has turned out a just one. I always was convinced that those princes who received other presents from Bonaparte could have no plausible excuse to decline his ribands, crosses and stars. But who could have presumed to think that, in return for these blood-stained baubles, they would have sacrificed those honourable and dignified ornaments which, for ages past, have been the exclusive distinction of what birth had exalted, virtue made eminent, talents conspicuous, honour illustrious, or valour meritorious? Who would have dared to say that the Prussian Eagle and the Spanish Golden Fleece should thus be prostituted, thus polluted? I do not mean by this remark to throw any blame on the conferring those and other orders on Napoleon Bonaparte, or even on his brothers; I know it is usual, between *legitimate* sovereigns in alliance, sometimes to exchange their knighthoods; but to debase royal orders so much as to present them to a Cambacérès, a Talleyrand, a Fouché, a Bernadotte, a Fesch, and other vile and criminal wretches, I do not deny to have excited my astonishment, as well as my indignation. What *honest*—I do not say what *noble*—subjects of Prussia, or of Spain, will hereafter think themselves rewarded for their loyalty, industry, patriotism or zeal, when they remember that their Sovereigns have nothing to give but what the rebel has obtained, the robber worn, the murderer villified and the regicide debased?

The number of grand officers of the Legion of Honour does not yet amount to more than eighty, according to a list *circulated at Milan last spring*, of which I have seen a copy. Of these grand officers, three had been shoemakers, two tailors, four bakers, four barbers, six friars, eight abbés, six officers, three pedlars, three chandlers, seven drummers, sixteen soldiers, and eight regicides; four were lawful Kings, and the six others, Electors or Princes of the most ancient houses in Europe. I have looked over our own official list, and, as far as I know, the calculation is exact, both with regard to the number and to the quality.

This new institution of knighthood produced a singular effect on my vain and giddy countrymen, who, for twelve years before, had scarcely seen a star or a riband, except those of foreign ambassadors, who were frequently insulted when wearing them. It became now the fashion to be a knight, and those who really were not so, put pinks, or rather blooms, or flowers of a darker red, in their buttonholes, so as to resemble, and to be taken at a distance for, the red ribands of the members of the Legion of Honour.

A man of the name of Villeaume, an engraver by profession, took advantage of this knightly fashion and mania, and sold for four louis d'or, not only the stars, but pretended letters of knighthood, said to be procured by his connection with persons of the household of the Emperor. In a month's time, according to a register kept by him, he had made twelve hundred and fifty knights. When his fraud was discovered, he was already out of the way, safe with his money; and, notwithstanding the researches of the police, has not since been taken.

A person, calling himself Baron von Rinken, a subject

13—2

and an agent of one of the many Princes of Hohenlohe, according to his own assertion, arrived here with real letters and patents of knighthood, which he offered for sale for three hundred livres—£12. The stars of this Order were as large as the star of the grand officers of the Legion of Honour, and nearly resembled it; but the ribands were of a different colour. He had already disposed of a dozen of these stars, when he was taken up by the police and shut up in the Temple, where he still remains. Four other agents of inferior petty German princes have also been arrested for offering the Orders of their Sovereigns for sale.

A Captain Rouvais, who received six wounds in his campaign under Pichegru in 1794, wore the star of the Legion of Honour without being nominated a knight. He has been tried by a military commission, deprived of his pension, and condemned to four years' imprisonment in irons. He proved that he had presented fourteen petitions to Bonaparte for obtaining this mark of distinction, but in vain; while hundreds of others, who had hardly seen an enemy, or, at the most, made but one campaign, or been once wounded, had succeeded in their demands. As soon as sentence had been pronounced against him, he took a small pistol from his pocket, and shot himself through the head, saying, "Some one else will soon do the same for Bonaparte."

A cobbler, of the name of Matthieu, either in a fit of madness or from hatred to the new order of things, decorated himself with the large riband of the Legion of Honour, and had an old star fastened on his coat. Thus accoutred, he went into the Palais Royal, in the middle of the day, got upon a chair, and began to speak to his audience of the absurdity of true republicans not being on a level, even under an Emperor, and putting on, like him, all his ridiculous ornaments. "We are here," said he, "either all grand officers, or there exist no grand officers at all; we have all fought and paid for liberty, and for the Revolution, as much as Bonaparte, and have, therefore, the same right and claim with him." Here a police agent and some gendarmes interrupted his *eloquence* by taking him into custody. When Fouché asked him what he meant by such rebellious behaviour, he replied "that it was only a trial to see whether destiny had intended him to become an Emperor, or to remain a cobbler. On the next day he was shot as a conspirator. I saw the unfortunate man in the Palais Royal; his eyes looked wild, and his words were often incoherent. He was certainly a subject more deserving a place in a mad-house than in a tomb.

Cambacérès has been severely reprimanded by the Emperor for showing too much partiality for the Royal Prussian Black Eagle, by wearing it in preference to the

Imperial Legion of Honour. He was given to understand that, except for four days in the year, the imperial etiquette did not permit any subjects to display their knighthood of the Prussian Order. In Madame Bonaparte's last drawing-room, before His Imperial Majesty set out for the Rhine, he was ornamented with the Spanish, Neapolitan, Prussian and Portuguese Orders, together with those of the French Legion of Honour, and of the Italian Iron Crown. I have seen the Emperor Paul, who was also an amateur of ribands and stars, but never with so many at once. I have just heard that the Grand Master of Malta has presented Napoleon with the Grand Cross of the Maltese Order. This is certainly a negative compliment to him, who, in July, 1798, officially declared to his then sectaries, the Turks and Mussulmans, "that the Grand Master, Commanders, Knights and Order of Malta *existed no more.*"

I have heard it related for a certainty, among our fashionable ladies, that the Empress of the French also intends to institute a new order of female knighthood, *not of honour,* but of *confidence;* of which all our Court ladies, all the wives of our generals, public functionaries, &c., are to be members. The Imperial Princesses of the Bonaparte family are to be hereditary grand officers, together with as many foreign empresses, queens, princesses, countesses and baronesses as can be bayoneted into this revolutionary sisterhood. Had the Continent remained tranquil, it would already have been officially announced by a Senatus Consultum. I should suppose that Madame Bonaparte, with her splendid Court, and brilliant retinue of German princes and electors at Strasburg, need only say the word to find hundreds of princely recruits for her knighthood *in petto*. Her mantle, as a Grand Mistress of the Order of CONFIDENCE, has been already embroidered at Lyons, and those who have seen it assert that it is truly superb. The diamonds of the star on the mantle are valued at six hundred thousand livres—£25,000.

LETTER LXVI

PARIS, *October*, 1805.

MY LORD,—Since Bonaparte's departure for Germany, fifteen individuals have been brought here chained from La Vendée and the Western Departments, and are imprisoned in the Temple. Their crime is not exactly known, but private letters from those countries relate that they were recruiting for another insurrection, and that some of them were entrusted as ambassadors from their discontented countrymen to Louis XVIII. to ask for his return to France, and for the assistance of Russia, Sweden and England to support his claims.

These are, however, reports to which I do not affix much credit. Had the prisoners in the Temple been guilty, or only *accused* of such crimes, they would long ago have been tortured, tried and executed, or executed without a trial. I suppose them mere hostages arrested by our Government, as security for the tranquillity of the Chouan Departments during our armies' occupation elsewhere. We have, nevertheless, two movable columns of six thousand men each in the country, or in its vicinity, and it would be not only impolitic, but a cruelty, to engage or allure the unfortunate people of these wretched countries into any plots, which, situated as affairs now are, would be productive of great and certain evil to them, without even the probability of any benefit to the cause of royalty and of the Bourbons. I do not mean to say that there are not those who rebel against Bonaparte's tyranny, or that the Bourbons have no friends; on the contrary, the latter are not few, and the former very numerous. But a kind of apathy, the effect of unavailing resistance to usurpation and oppression, has seized on most minds, and annihilated what little remained of our never very great public spirit. We are tired of everything, even of our existence, and care no more whether we are governed by a Maximilian Robespierre or by a Napoleon Bonaparte, by a Barras or by Louis XVIII. Except, perhaps, among the military, or among some ambitious schemers, remnants of former factions, I do not believe a Moreau, a Macdonald, a Lucien Bonaparte, or any person exiled by the Emperor, and formerly popular, could collect fifty trusty conspirators in all France; at least, as long as our armies are victorious, and organized in their present formidable manner. Should anything happen to our present chief, an impulse may be given to the minds now sunk down, and raise our characters from their present torpid state. But until such an event, we shall remain as we are, indolent but submissive, sacrificing our children and treasures for a cause we detest, and for a man we abhor. I am sorry to say it, but it certainly does no honour to my nation when one million desperadoes of civil and military banditti are suffered to govern, tyrannize and pillage, at their ease and undisturbed, thirty millions of people, to whom their past crimes are known, and who have every reason to apprehend their future wickedness.

This astonishing *resignation* (if I can call it so, and if it does not deserve a worse name), is so much the more incomprehensible, as the poverty of the higher and middle-classes is as great as the misery of the people, and except those employed under Bonaparte, and some few upstart contractors or army commissaries, the greatest privations must be submitted to in order to pay the enormous taxes and make a decent appearance. I know families of five, six and seven persons, who formerly were wealthy, and now have for a scanty subsistence an income of twelve or eighteen hundred livres — £50 or £75 — per year, with which they are obliged to live as they can, being deprived of all the resource that elsewhere labour offers to the industrious, and all the succours compassion bestows on the necessitous. You know that here all trade and all commerce are at a stand or destroyed, and the hearts of our modern rich are as unfeeling as their manners are vulgar and brutal.

A family of *ci-devant* nobles of my acquaintance, once possessing a revenue of one hundred and fifty thousand livres — £6,300 — subsist now on fifteen hundred livres £63 — per year; and this sum must support six individuals — the father and mother, with four children! It does so, indeed, by an arrangement of only one poor meal in the day; a dinner four times, and a supper three times, in the week. They endure their distress with tolerable cheerfulness, though in the same street, where they occupy the garrets of a house, resides, in an elegant hotel, a man who was once their groom, but who is now a tribune, and has within these last twelve years, as a conventional deputy, amassed, in his mission to Brabant and Flanders, twelve millions of livres -£500,000. He has *kindly* let my friend understand that his youngest daughter might be received as a chambermaid to his wife, *being informed that she has got a good education*. All the four daughters are good musicians, good drawers, and very able with their needles. By their talents they supported their parents and themselves during their emigration in Germany; but here these are of but little use or advantage. Those upstarts who want instruction or works of this sort, apply to the first most renowned and fashionable masters or mistresses: while others, and those the greatest number, cannot afford even to pay the inferior ones and the most cheap. This family is one of the many that regret having returned from their emigration. But, you may ask, why do they not go back again to Germany? First, it would expose them to suspicion, and, perhaps, to ruin, were they to demand passes; and if this danger or difficulty were removed, they have no money for such a long journey.

But this sort of penury and wretchedness is also common with the families of the former wealthy merchants and tradesmen. Paper money, a maximum and requisitions, have reduced those that did not share in the crimes and pillage of the Revolution, as much as the proscribed nobility. And, contradictory as it may seem, the number of persons employed in commercial speculations has more than tripled since we experienced a general stagnation of trade, the consequence of war, of want of capital, protection, encouragement, and confidence; but one of the magazines of 1789 contained more goods and merchandize than twenty modern magazines put together. The expenses of these new merchants are, however, much greater than sixteen years ago, the profit less, and the credit still less than the profit. Hence numerous bankruptcies, frauds, swindling, forgeries, and other evils of immorality, extravagance and misery. The fair and honest dealers suffer most from the intrusion of these infamous speculators, who —expecting, like other vile men wallowing in wealth under their eyes, to make rapid fortunes, and to escape detection as well as punishment—commit crimes to soothe disappointment. Nothing is done but for ready money, and even bankers' bills, or bills accepted by bankers, are not taken in payment before the signatures are avowed by the parties concerned. You can easily conceive what confusion, what expenses, and what loss of time these precautions must occasion; but the numerous forgeries and fabrications have made them absolutely necessary.

The farmers and land-holders are better off, but they also complain of the heavy taxes, and low price paid for what they bring to the market, which frequently, for want of ready money, remains long unsold. They take nothing but cash in payment; for, notwithstanding the endeavours of our Government, the notes of the Bank of France have never been in circulation among them. They have also been subject to losses by the fluctuation of paper money, by extortions, requisitions and by the maximum. In this class of my countrymen remains still some little national spirit and some independence of character; but these are far from being favourable to Bonaparte, or to the Imperial Government, which the yearly increase of taxes, and, above all, the conscription, have rendered extremely odious. You may judge of the great difference in the taxation of lands and landed property now and under our kings, when I inform you that a friend of mine, who, in 1792, possessed, in one of the Western Departments, twenty-one farms, paid less in contribution for them all than he does now for the three farms he has recovered from the wreck of his fortune.

LETTER LXVII

PARIS, *October*, 1805.

MY LORD,—In a military empire, ruled by a military despot, it is a necessary policy that the education of youth should also be military. In all our public schools or prytanees, a boy, from the moment of entering, is registered in a company, and regularly drilled, exercised and reviewed, punished for neglect or fault according to martial law, and advanced if displaying genius or application. All our private schools that wish for the protection of Government are forced to submit to the same military rules, and, therefore, most of our conscripts, so far from being recruits, are fit for any service as soon as put into requisition. The fatal effects to the independence of Europe to be dreaded from this sole innovation, I apprehend, have been too little considered by other nations. A great Power, that can, without obstacle, and with but little expense, in four weeks increase its disposable military force from one hundred and twenty to one hundred and eighty thousand young men, accustomed to military duty from their youth, *must finally become the master of all other or rival Powers*, and dispose at leisure of empires, kingdoms, principalities and republics. —Nothing can save them but the adoption of similar measures for their preservation as have been adopted for their subjugation.

When *l'État Militaire* for the year 13 (a work containing the official statement of our military forces) was presented to Bonaparte by Berthier, the latter said, "Sire, I lay before your Majesty the book of the destiny of the world, which your hands direct as the sovereign guide of the armies of your empire." This compliment is a truth, and therefore no flattery. It might as justly have been addressed to a Moreau, a Macdonald, a Le Courbe, or to any other general, as to Bonaparte, because a superior number of well disciplined troops, let them be well or even indifferently commanded, will defeat those inferior in number. Three to one would even overpower an army of giants. Add to it the unity of plans, of dispositions, and of execution, which Bonaparte enjoys exclusively over such a great number of troops, while ten, or perhaps fifty, will direct or contradict every movement of his opponents. I tremble when I meditate on Berthier's assertion; may I never live to see it realized, and to see all hitherto independent nations prostrated acknowledge that Bonaparte and destiny are the same, and the same distributor of good and evil.

One of the bad consequences of this our military education of youth is a total absence of all religious and moral lessons. Arnaud had, last August, the courage to complain of this infamous neglect, in the National Institute. "The youth," said he, "receive no other instruction but lessons to march, to fire, to bow, to dance, to sit, to lie and to impose with a good grace. I do not ask for Spartans or Romans, but we want Athenians, and our schools are only forming Sybarites." Within twenty-four hours afterwards, Arnaud was visited by a police agent, accompanied by two gendarmes, with an order signed by Fouché, which condemned him to reside at Orleans, and not to return to Paris without the permission of the Government, a punishment regarded here as very *moderate* for such an indiscreet zeal.

A schoolmaster at Auteuil, near this capital, of the name of Gouron, had a private seminary, organized upon the footing of our former colleges. In some few months he was offered more pupils than he well could attend to, and his house shortly became very fashionable, even for our upstarts, who sent their children there in preference. He was ordered before Fouché last Christmas, and commanded to change the hours hitherto employed in teaching religion and morals, to a military exercise and instruction, as both more *necessary* and more *salubrious* for French youth. Having replied that such an alteration was contrary to his plan and agreement with the parents of his scholars, the minister stopped him short by telling him that he *must* obey what had been prescribed by Government, or stand the consequences of his refractory spirit. Having consulted with his friends and patrons, he divided the hours, and gave half of the time usually allotted to religion or morality to the study of military exercise. His pupils, however, remained obstinate, broke the drum, and tore and burnt the colours he had bought. As this was not his fault, he did not expect any further disturbance, particularly after having reported to the police both his obedience and the unforeseen result. But last March his house was suddenly surrounded in the night by gendarmes, and some police agents entered it. All the boys were ordered to dress and to pack up their effects, and to follow the gendarmes to several other schools, where the Government had placed them, and of which their parents would be informed. Gouron, his wife, four ushers and six servants, were all arrested and carried to the police office, where Fouché, after reproaching them for their fanatical behaviour, as he termed it, told them, as they were so fond of teaching religious and moral duties, a suitable situation had been provided for them in Cayenne, where the negroes stood sadly in need of their early arrival, for which reason they would all set out on that very morning for Rochefort. When Gouron asked what was to become of his property, furniture, &c., he was told that his house was intended by Government for a preparatory school, and would, with its contents, be purchased, and the amount paid him in lands in Cayenne. It is not necessary to say that this example of imperial *justice* had the desired effect on all other refractory private schoolmasters.

The parents of Gouron's pupils were, with a severe reprimand, informed where their sons had been placed, and where they would be educated in a manner agreeable to the Emperor, who *recommended* them not to remove them, without a previous notice to the police. A hatter, of the name of Maille, however, ordered his son home, because he had been sent to a dearer school than the former. In his turn he was carried before the police, and, after a short examination of a quarter-of-an-hour, was permitted, with his wife and two children, to join their friend Gouron at Rochefort, and to settle with him at Cayenne, where lands would also be given him for his property in France. These particulars were related to me by a neighbour whose son had, for two years previous to this, been under Gouron's care, but who was now among those placed out by our Government. The boy's present master, he said, was a man of a notoriously bad and immoral character; but he was intimidated, and weak enough to remain contented, preferring, no doubt, his personal safety to the future happiness of his child. In your country, you little comprehend what a *valuable* instrument terror has been in the hands of our rulers since the Revolution, and how often fear has been mistaken abroad for affection and content.

All these *minutiæ* and petty vexations, but great oppressions, of petty tyrants, you may easily guess, take up a great deal of time, and that, therefore, a minister of police, though the most powerful, is also the most occupied of his colleagues. So he certainly is, but, last year, a new organization of this ministry was regulated by Bonaparte ; and Fouché was allowed, as assistants, four counsellors of state, and an augmentation of sixty-four police commissaries. The French empire was then divided into four *arrondissements*, with regard to the general police, not including Paris and its vicinity, inspected by a prefect of police under the minister. Of the first of these *arrondissements*, the counsellor of state, Real, is a kind of deputy minister ; the counsellor of state, Miot, is the same of the second ; the counsellor of state, Pelet de la Lozére, of the third ; and the counsellor of state, Dauchy, of the fourth. The secret police agents, formerly called *spies*, were also considerably increased.

LETTER LXVIII

PARIS, *October*, 1805.

MY LORD,—Before Bonaparte set out for the Rhine, the Pope's Nuncio was for the *first time* publicly rebuked by him in Madame Bonaparte's drawing-room, and ordered *loudly* to write to Rome and tell his Holiness to think himself fortunate in continuing to govern the Ecclesiastical States, without interfering with the ecclesiastical arrangements that might be thought necessary or proper by the Government in France.

Bonaparte's policy is to promote among the first dignitaries of the Gallican Church the brothers or relatives of his civil or military supporters; Cambacérès' brother is, therefore, an archbishop and cardinal, and one of Le Brun's, and two of Berthier's cousins are bishops. As, however, the relatives of these senators, ministers or generals, have, like themselves, figured in many of the scandalous and blasphemous scenes of the Revolution, the Pope has sometimes hesitated about sanctioning their promotions. This was the case last summer, when General Dessolles' brother was transferred from the bishopric of Digne to that of

Chambery, and Bonaparte nominated for his successor the brother of General Miollis, who was a curate of Brignoles, in the diocese of Aix. This curate had not only been one of the first to throw up his letters of priesthood at the Jacobin club at Aix, but had also sacrilegiously denied the divinity of the Christian religion, and proposed, in imitation of Parisian atheists, the worship of a Goddess of Reason in a common prostitute with whom he lived. The notoriety of these abominations made even his parishioners at Brignoles unwilling to go to church, and to regard him as their pastor, though several of them had been imprisoned, fined, and even transported as fanatics, or as refractory.

During the negotiation with Cardinal Fesch last year, the Pope had been promised, among other things, that, for the future, his conscience should not be wounded by having presented to him for the prelacy any persons but those of the purest morals of the French empire; and that all his objections should be attended to, in case of promotions: his scruples removed, or his refusal submitted to. When Cardinal Fesch demanded his Holiness's Bull for the curate Miollis, the Cardinal secretary of state, Gonsalvi, showed no less than twenty acts of apostasy and blasphemy, which made him unworthy of such a dignity. To this was replied that, having obtained an indulgence *in toto* for what was past, he was a proper subject: above all, as he had the protection of the Emperor of the French. The Pope's Nuncio here then addressed himself to our minister of the ecclesiastical department, Portalis, who advised him not to speak to Bonaparte of a matter upon which his mind had been made up; he, nevertheless, demanded an audience, and it was in consequence of this request that he, in his turn, became acquainted with the new imperial etiquette and new imperial jargon towards the representatives of Sovereigns. On the same evening the Nuncio expedited a courier to Rome, and I have heard to-day that the nomination of Miollis is confirmed by the Pope.

From this relatively trifling occurrence, his Holiness might judge of the intention of our Government to adhere to its other engagements; but at Rome, as well as in most other Continental capitals, the Sovereign is the dupe of the perversity of his counsellors and ministers, who are the tools, and not seldom the pensioners, of the Cabinet of St. Cloud.

But in the kingdom of Italy the parishes and dioceses are, if possible, still worse served than in this country. Some of the bishops there, after having done duty in the National Guards, worn the Jacobin cap, and fought against their lawful Prince, now live in open adultery; and, from their intrigues, are the terror of all the married part of their flock. The Bishop of Pavia keeps the wife of a merchant, by whom he has two children; and, that the public may not be mistaken as to their real father, the merchant received a sum of money to establish himself at Brescia, and has not seen his wife for these two years past. General Gourion, who was last spring in Italy, has assured me that he read the advertisement of a curate after his concubine, who had eloped with another curate; and that the police minister at Milan openly licensed women to be the *housekeepers* of priests.

A grand vicar, Sarini, at Bologna, was, in 1796, a friar, but relinquished then the convent for the tent, and exchanged the breviary for the musket. He married a nun of one cloister, from whom he procured a divorce in a month, to unite himself with an abbess of another, deserted by him in her turn for the wife of an innkeeper, who robbed and eloped from her husband. Last spring he returned to the bosom of the Church, and, by making our Empress a present of a valuable diamond cross, of which he had pillaged the statue of a Madonna, he obtained the dignity of a grand vicar, to the great edification, no doubt, of all those who had seen him before the altar or in the camp, at the brothel or in the hospital.

Another grand vicar of the same bishop, in the same city, of the name of Rami, has two of his illegitimate children as singing-boys in the same cathedral where he officiates as a priest. Their mother is dead, but her daughter, by another priest, is now their father's mistress. This incestuous commerce is so little concealed that the girl does the honours of the grand vicar's house, and, with *naïveté* enough, tells the guests and visitors of her *happiness* in having succeeded her mother. I have this anecdote from an officer who heard her make use of that expression.

In France our priests, I fear, are equally as debauched and unprincipled; but, in yielding to their vicious propensities, they take care to save the appearance of virtue, and though their guilt is the same, the scandal is less. Bonaparte pretends to be severe against all those ecclesiastics who are accused of any irregularities after having made their peace with the Church. A curate of Picardy, suspected of gallantry, and another of Normandy, accused of inebriety, were last month, without further trial or ceremony than the report of the minister Portalis, delivered over to Fouché, who transported them to Cayenne, after they had been stripped of their gowns. At the same time, Cardinal Cambacérès and Cardinal Fesch, equally notorious for their excesses, were taken no notice of, except that they were laughed at in our Court circles.

I am, almost every day, more and more convinced that our Government is totally indifferent about what becomes of our religious establishment when the present race of priests is extinguished; which, in the course of nature, must happen in less than thirty years. Our military system and our military education discourage all young men from entering into orders; while, at the same time, the army is both more honourable and more profitable than the Church. Already we want curates, though several have been imported from Germany and Spain, and, in some departments, four, and even six, parishes have only one curate to serve them all. The bishops exhort, and the parents advise their children to study theology; but then the law of conscription obliges the student of theology, as well as the student of philosophy, to march together: and, when once in the ranks, and accustomed to the licentiousness of a military life, they are either unwilling, unfit, or unworthy to return to anything else. The Pope, with all his entreaties, and with all his prayers, was unable to procure an exception from the conscription of young men preparing themselves for priesthood. Bonaparte always answered: "Holy Father, were I to consent to your demand, I should soon have an army of priests, instead of an army of soldiers." Our Emperor is not unacquainted with the real character and spirit of his *Volunteers*. When the Pope represented the danger of religion expiring in France, for want of priests to officiate at the altars, he was answered that Bonaparte, at the beginning of his consulate, found neither altars nor priests in France; that if his reign survived the latter, the former would always be standing, and survive his reign. He trusted that the chief of the Church would prevent them from being deserted. He assured him that when once he had restored the *liberties* of the seas, and an *uninterrupted* tranquillity on the Continent, he should attend more, and perhaps entirely, to the affairs of the Church. He consented, however, that the Pope might institute, in the Ecclesiastical States, a seminary for two hundred young Frenchmen, whom he would exempt from military conscription. This is the stock from which our Church establishment is to be supplied!

LETTER LXIX

PARIS, *October*, 1805.

MY LORD,—The short journey of Count de Haugwitz to Vienna, and the long stay of our Imperial Grand Marshal, Duroc, at Berlin, had already caused here many speculations, not quite corresponding with the views and, perhaps, interests of our Court, when our violation of the Prussian territory made our courtiers exclaim, "This act proves that the Emperor of the French is in a situation to bid defiance to all the world, and, therefore, no longer courts the neutrality of a Prince whose power is merely artificial; who has indemnities to restore, but no delicacy, no regard to claims." Such was the language of those very men, who, a month before, declared "that His Prussian Majesty held the balance of peace or war in his hands; that he was in a position in which no Prussian Monarch ever was before; that while his neutrality preserved the tranquillity of the North of Germany, the South of Europe would soon be indebted to his powerful mediation for the return of peace."

The real cause of this alteration in our courtiers'

political jargon has not yet been known: but I think it may easily be discovered without any official publication. Bonaparte had the adroitness to cajole the Cabinet of Berlin into his interest, in the first month of his consulate, notwithstanding his own critical situation, as well as the critical situation of France; and he has ever since taken care both to attach it to his triumphal car and to inculpate it indirectly in his outrages and violations. Convinced, as he thought, of the selfishness which guided all its resolutions, all his attacks and invasions against the law of nations, or independence of states, were either preceded or followed with some offers of aggrandizement, of indemnity, of subsidy, or of alliance. His political intriguers were generally more successful in Prussia than his military heroes in crossing the Rhine or the Elbe, in laying the Hanse Towns under contribution, or in occupying Hanover; or, rather, all these acts of violence and injustice were merely the effects of his ascendancy in Prussia. When it is, besides, remembered what provinces Prussia accepted from his bounty, what exchange of presents, of ribands, of private letters passed between Napoleon the First and Frederick William III., between the Empress of the French and the Queen of Prussia, it is not surprising if the Cabinet of St. Cloud thought itself sure of the submission of the Cabinet of Berlin, and did not esteem it enough to fear it, or to think that it would have spirit enough to resent, or even honour to feel, the numerous provocations offered.

Whatever Bonaparte and Talleyrand write or assert to the contrary, their gifts are only the wages of their contempt, and they despise more that state they thus reward than those nations at whose expense they are liberal, and with whose spoil they delude selfishness or meanness into their snares. The more legitimate Sovereigns descend from their true dignity, and a liberal policy, the nearer they approach the baseness of usurpation and the Machiavellism of rebellion. Like other upstarts, they never suffer an equal. If you do not keep yourself above them, they will crush you beneath them. If they have no reason to fear you, they will create some quarrel to destroy you.

It is said here that Duroc's journey to Berlin was *merely* to demand a passage for the French troops through the Prussian territory in Franconia, and to prevent the Russian troops from passing through the Prussian territory in Poland. This request is such as might have been expected from our Emperor and his minister. Whether, however, the tone in which this curious negotiation with a *neutral* power was begun, or that, at last, the generosity of the Russian Monarch awakened a sense of duty in the Cabinet of Berlin, the arrival of our pacific envoy was immediately followed with warlike preparations. Fortunate, indeed, was it for Prussia to have resorted to her military strength instead of trusting any longer to our friendly assurances. The disasters that have since befallen the Austrian armies in Suabia, partly occasioned by our forced marches through *neutral* Prussia, would otherwise soon have been felt in Westphalia, in Brandenburg and in Pomerania. But should His Prussian Majesty not order his troops to act in conjunction with Russia, Austria, England and Sweden, and *that very soon*, all efforts against Bonaparte will be vain, as those troops which have dispersed the Austrians and repulsed the Russians will be more than equal to master the Prussians, and one campaign may be sufficient to convince the Prussian ministers of their folly and errors for years, and to punish them for their ignorance or selfishness.

Some preparations made in silence by the Marquis de Lucchesini, his affected absence from some of our late Court circles, and the number of spies who now are watching his hotel and his steps, seem to indicate that Prussia is tired of its impolitic neutrality, and inclined to join the confederacy against France. At the last assembly at our Prince Cambacérès', a rumour circulated that preliminary articles for an offensive alliance with your country had already been signed by the Prussian minister, Baron

Hardenberg, on one side, and by your minister to the Court of Berlin on the other: according to which you were to take sixty thousand Prussians and twelve thousand Hessians into your pay, for five years certain. A courier from Duroc was said to have brought this news, which at first made some impression, but it wore away by degrees; and our Government, to judge from the expressions of persons in its confidence, seems more to court than to fear a rupture with Prussia. Indeed, besides all other reasons to carry on a war in the North of Europe, Bonaparte's numerous new and young generals are impatient to enrich themselves, as Italy, Switzerland, Holland and the South of Germany are almost exhausted.

LETTER LXX

PARIS, *October* 1805.

MY LORD,—The provocations of our Government must have been extraordinary indeed, when they were able to awaken the Cabinet of Berlin from its long and incomprehensible infatuation of trusting to the friendly intentions of *honest* Talleyrand, and to the disinterested policy of our *generous* Bonaparte. To judge its intents from its acts, the *favour* of the Cabinet of St. Cloud was not only its wish but its want. You must remember that, last year, besides his ordinary ambassador, Lucchesini, His Prussian Majesty was so ill advised as to despatch General Knobelsdorff as his extra representative, to assist at Napoleon's coronation, a degradation of lawful sovereignty to which even the Court of Naples, though surrounded with our troops, refused to subscribe; and, so late as last June, the same Knobelsdorff did, in the name of his Prince, the honours at the reviews near Magdeburg, to all the generals of our army in Hanover who chose to attend there. On this occasion the King lodged in a farm-house, the Queen in the house of the curate of Koestelith, while our *sans-culotte* officers, Bernadotte & Co., were quartered and treated in style at the castle of Putzbull, fitted up for their accommodation. This was certainly very hospitable, and very *civil*, but it was neither prudent nor politic. Upstarts, experiencing such a reception from princes, are convinced that they are dreaded, because they know that they have not merit to be esteemed.

Do not confound this Knobelsdorff with the late field-marshal of that name, who, in 1796, answered to a request which our then ambassador at Berlin (Abbé Siéyes) had made to be introduced to him, NON ET SANS PHRASE, the very words this regicide used when he sat in judgment on his King, and voted LA MORT ET SANS PHRASE. This Knobelsdorff is a very different character. He pretends to be equally conspicuous in the cabinet as in the field, in the boudoir as in the study. A demi-philosopher, a demi-savant, a demi-gallant and a demi-politician, constitute, all taken together, nothing except an insignificant courtier. I do not know whether he was among those Prussian officers who, in 1798, CRIED when it was inserted in the public prints that the Grand Bonaparte had been killed in an insurrection at Cairo, but of this I am certain, that were Knobelsdorff to survive Napoleon the First, none of His Imperial Majesty's own dutiful subjects would mourn him more sincerely than this subject of the King of Prussia.

He is said to possess a great share of the confidence of his King, who has already employed him in several diplomatic missions. The principal and most requisite qualities in a negotiator are political information, inviolable fidelity, penetrating but unbiased judgment, a dignified firmness and condescending manners. I have not been often enough in the society of General Knobelsdorff to assert whether nature and education have destined him to illumine or to cloud the Prussian monarchy.

I have already mentioned in a former letter that it was Count de Haugwitz who, in 1792, as Prussian ambassador at Vienna, arranged the treaty which then united the Austrian and Prussian Eagles against the Jacobin Cap of Liberty. It is now said in our diplomatic circle that his second mission to the same capital has for an object the renewal of these ties, which the Treaty of Basle dissolved; and that our Government, to impede his success, or to occasion his recall, before he could have time to conclude, had proposed to Prussia an annual subsidy of thirty millions of livres—£1,250,000—*which it intended to exact from Portugal for its neutrality.* The present respectable appearance of Prussia shows, however, that whether the mission of Haugwitz had the desired issue or not, His Prussian Majesty confides in his army in preference to our parchments.

Some of our politicians pretend that the present

minister of the foreign department in Prussia, Baron de
Hardenberg, is not such a friend of the system of neutrality
as his predecessor. All the transactions of his administration seem, nevertheless, to proclaim that, if he wished his
country to take an active part in the present conflict, it
would not have been against France, had she not begun
the attack with the invasion of Anspach and Bayreuth. Let
it be recollected that, since his ministry, Prussia has
acknowledged Bonaparte an Emperor of the French, has
exchanged orders with him, and has sent an extraordinary
ambassador to be present at his coronation—not common
compliments, even between Princes connected by the
nearest ties of friendship and consanguinity. Under his
administration, the Rhine has been passed to seize the
Duke of Enghien, and the Elbe to capture Sir George
Rumbold; the Hanse Towns have been pillaged, and
even Emden blockaded; and the representations against
all these outrages have neither been followed by public
reparation nor a becoming resentment; and was it not also
Baron de Hardenberg, who, on the 5th of April, 1795,
concluded at Basle that treaty to which we owe all our
conquests, and Germany and Italy all their disasters? It
is not probable that the parent of pacification will destroy
its own progeny, if self-preservation does not require it.

    Baron de Hardenberg is both a learned nobleman and

an enlightened statesman, and does equal honour both to his own rank and to the choice of his Prince. The late Frederick William II. nominated him a minister of state and a counsellor of his Cabinet. On the 26th of January, 1792, as a directorial minister, he took possession, in the name of the King of Prussia, of the Margravates of Anspach and Bayreuth, and the inhabitants swore before him, as their governor, their oaths of allegiance to their new Sovereign. He continued to reside, as a kind of viceroy, in these states until March, 1795, when he replaced Baron de Goltz as negotiator with our republican plenipotentiary in Switzerland; but, after settling all differences between Prussia and France, he returned to his former post at Anspach, where no complaints have been heard against his government.

The ambition of Baron de Hardenberg has always been to obtain the place he now occupies, and the study of his life has been to gain such information as would enable him to fill it with distinction. I have heard it said that in most countries he had for years kept and paid private agents, who regularly corresponded with him and sent him reports of what they heard or saw of political intrigue or machinations. One of these his agents I happened to meet with, in 1796, at Basle, and were I to conclude from what I observed in him, the minister has not been very judicious in his selection of private correspondents. Figure to yourself a bald-headed personage, about forty years of age, near seven feet high, deaf as a post, stammering and making convulsive efforts to express a sentence of five words, which, after all, his gibberish made unintelligible. His dress was as eccentric as his person was singular, and his manners corresponded with both. He called himself Baron de Bülow, and I saw him afterwards in the autumn of 1797, at Paris, with the same accoutrements and the same jargon, assuming an air of diplomatic mystery, even while displaying before me, in a coffee-house, his letters and instructions from his principal. As might be expected, he had the adroitness to get himself shut up in the Temple, where, I have been told, the generosity of your Sir Sidney Smith prevented him from starving.

No member of the foreign diplomatic corps here possesses either more knowledge or a longer experience, than the Prussian ambassador, Marquis de Lucchesini. He went, with several other *philosophers* of Italy, to admire the late hero of modern philosophy at Berlin, Frederick the Great, who received him well, caressed him often, but never trusted or employed him. I suppose it was not at the mention of the Marquis' name for the place of a governor of some province that this Monarch said, " My subjects of that province have always been dutiful : a philosopher shall never rule in my name but over people with whom I am discontented, or whom I intend to chastise." This Prince was not unacquainted with the morality of his sectaries.

During the latter part of the life of this King, the Marquis de Lucchesini was frequently of his literary and convivial parties; but he was neither his friend nor his favourite, but his listener. It was first under Frederick William II. that he began his diplomatic career, with an appointment as minister from Prussia to the late King of Poland. His first act in this post was a treaty signed on the 29th of March, 1790, with the King and Republic of Poland, which changed an elective monarchy into an hereditary one; but notwithstanding the Cabinet of Berlin had guaranteed this alteration, and the constitution decreed in consequence in 1791, three years afterwards Russian and Prussian bayonets annihilated both, and selfishness banished faith.

In July, 1790, he assisted as a Prussian plenipotentiary at the conferences at Reichenbach, together with the English and Dutch ambassadors, having for object a pacification between Austria and Turkey. In December of the same year he went with the same ministers to the Congress at Sistova, where, in May, 1791, he signed the Treaty of Peace between the Grand Seignior and the Emperor of Germany. In June, 1792, he was a second time sent as a minister to Warsaw, where he remained until January, 1793, when he was promoted to the post of ambassador at the Court of Vienna. He continued, however, to reside with His Prussian Majesty during the greatest part of the campaign on the Rhine, and signed, on the 24th of June, 1793, in the camp before Mentz, an offensive and defensive alliance with your Court; an alliance which Prussian policy respected not above eighteen months. In October, 1796, he requested his recall, but this his Sovereign refused, with the most gracious expressions; and he could not obtain it until March, 1797. Some disapprobation of the new political plan introduced by Count de Haugwitz in the Cabinet at Berlin is supposed to have occasioned his determination to retire from public employment. As he, however, continued to reside in the capital of Prussia, and, as many believed, secretly intrigued to appear again upon the scene, the nomination, in 1800, to his present important post was as much the consequence of his own desire as of the favour of his King.

The Marquis de Lucchesini lives here in great style at the beautiful Hôtel de l'Infantado, where his lady's routs, assemblies and circles are the resort of our most fashionable gentry. Madame de Lucchesini is more agreeable than handsome, more fit to shine at Berlin than at Paris; for though her manners are elegant, they want that ease, that finish which a German or Italian education cannot teach, nor a German or Italian society confer. To judge from the number of her admirers, she seems to know that she is married to a philosopher. Her husband was born at Lucca, in Italy, and is, therefore, at present a subject of Bonaparte's brother-in-law, Prince Baciocchi, to whom, when His Serene Highness was a marker at a billiard-table, I have had the honour of giving many a shilling, as well as many a box on the ear.

LETTER LXXI

Paris, *October*, 1805.

My Lord,—The unexampled cruelty of our Government to your countryman, Captain Wright, I have heard reprobated, even by some of our generals and public functionaries, as unjust as well as disgraceful. At a future General Congress, should ever Bonaparte suffer one to be convoked, except under his auspices and dictature, the distinction and treatment of prisoners of war require to be again regulated, that the valiant warrior may not for the future be confounded with, and treated as, a treacherous spy; nor innocent travellers, provided with regular passes, visiting a country either for business or for pleasure, be imprisoned, like men taken while combating with arms in their hands.

You remember, no doubt, from history, how many of our ships—that, during the reigns of George I. and II., carried to Ireland and Scotland, and landed there, the adherents and partisans of the House of Stuart—were captured on their return or on their passage: and that your Government never seized the commanders of these vessels, to confine them as state criminals, much less to torture or murder them in the Tower. If I am not mistaken, the whole squadron which, in 1745, carried the Pretender and his suite to Scotland, was taken by your cruisers; and the officers and men experienced no worse or different treatment than their fellow-prisoners of war: though the distance is immense between the crime of plotting against the lawful government of the Princes of the House of Brunswick, and the attempt to disturb the usurpation of an upstart of the *House* of Bonaparte. But, even during the last war, how many of our ships of the line, frigates and cutters, did you not take, which had landed rebels in Ireland, emissaries in Scotland, and malefactors in Wales; and yet your generosity prevented you from retaliating, even at the time when your Sir Sidney Smith, and this same unfortunate Captain Wright, were confined in our state prison of the Temple! It is with governments as with individuals, they ought to be just before they are generous. Had you in 1797, or in 1798, not endured our outrages so patiently, you would not now have to lament, nor we to blush for, the untimely end of Captain Wright.

From the last time that this officer had appeared before the criminal tribunal which condemned Georges and Moreau, his fate was determined on by our Government. His firmness offended, and his patriotism displeased; and as he seemed to possess the confidence of his own Government, it was judged that he was in its secrets; it was, therefore, resolved that, if he refused to become a traitor, he should perish a victim. Desmarets, Fouché's private secretary, who is also the secretary of the secret and *haute* police, therefore ordered him to another private interrogatory. Here he was offered a considerable sum of money, and the rank of an admiral in our service, if he would divulge what he knew of the plans of his Government, of its connections with the discontented in this country, and of its means of keeping up a correspondence with them. He replied, as might have been expected, with indignation to such offers and to such proposals, but as they were frequently repeated with new allurements, he concluded with remaining silent and giving no answers at all. He was then told that the torture would soon restore him his voice, and some select gendarmes seized him and laid him on the rack; there he uttered no complaint, not even a sigh, though instruments the most diabolical were employed, and pains the most acute must have been endured. When threatened that he should expire in torments, he said, "I do not fear to die, because my country will avenge my murder, while my God receives my soul." During the two hours of the first day that he was stretched on the rack, his left arm and right leg were broken, and his nails torn from the toes of both his feet: he then passed into the hands of a surgeon, and was under his care for five weeks, but before he was perfectly cured, he was carried to another private interrogatory, at which, besides Desmarets, Fouché and Real were present.

The minister of police now informed him that, from the mutilated state of his body, and from the sufferings he had gone through, he must be convinced that it was not the intention of the French Government ever to restore him to his native country, where he might relate occurrences which the *policy* of France required to be buried in oblivion ; he, therefore, had no choice between serving the Emperor of the French, or perishing within the walls of the prison where he was confined. He replied that he was resigned to his destiny, and would die as he had lived, faithful to his King and to his country.

The man in the full possession of his mental qualities and corporeal strength is, in most cases, very different from that unfortunate being whose mind is enervated by sufferings and whose body is weakened by wants. For five months Captain Wright had seen only gaolers, spies, tyrants, executioners, fetters, racks and other tortures ; and for five weeks his food had been bread and his drink water. The man who, thus situated and thus perplexed, preserves his native dignity and innate sentiments, is more worthy of monuments, statues or altars than either the legislator, the victor or the saint.

This interrogatory was the last undergone by Captain Wright. He was then again stretched on the rack, and what is called by our regenerators the INFERNAL torments, were inflicted on him. After being pinched with red-hot irons all over his body, brandy, mixed with gunpowder, was infused in the numerous wounds and set fire to several times until nearly burned to the bones. In the convulsions, the consequence of these terrible sufferings, he is said to have bitten off a part of his tongue, though, as before, no groans were heard. As life still remained he was again put under the care of his former surgeon; but, as he was exceedingly exhausted, a spy, in the dress of a Protestant clergyman, presented himself as if to read prayers with him. Of this offer he accepted; but when this man began to ask some insidious questions, he cast on him a look of contempt and never spoke to him more. At last, seeing no means to obtain any information from him, a mameluke last week strangled him in his bed. Thus expired a hero whose fate has excited more compassion, and whose character has received more admiration here, than any of our *great* men who have fallen fighting for our Emperor. Captain Wright has diffused new rays of renown and glory on the British name, from his tomb as well as from his dungeon.

You have certainly a right to call me to an account for all the particulars I have related of this scandalous and abominable transaction, and, though I cannot absolutely guarantee the truth of the narration, I am perfectly satisfied of it myself, and I hope to explain myself to your satisfaction. Your unfortunate countryman was attended by and under the care of a surgeon of the name of Vaugeard, who gained his confidence, and was worthy of it, though employed in that infamous gaol. Either from disgust of life, or from attachment to Captain Wright, he survived him only twelve hours, during which he wrote the shocking details I have given you, and sent them to three of the members of the foreign diplomatic corps, with a prayer to have them forwarded to Sir Sidney Smith or to Mr. Windham, that those his friends might be informed that, to his last moment, Captain Wright was worthy of their protection and kindness. From one of those ministers I have obtained the original in Vaugeard's own handwriting.

I know that Bonaparte and Talleyrand promised the release of Captain Wright to the Spanish ambassador; but, at that time, he had already suffered once on the rack, and this liberality on their part was merely a trick to impose upon the credulity of the Spaniard or to get rid of his importunities. Had it been otherwise, Captain Wright, like Sir George Rumbold, would himself have been the first to announce in your country the recovery of his liberty.

LETTER LXXII

PARIS, *October*, 1805.

MY LORD,—Should Bonaparte again return here victorious, and a pacificator, great changes in our internal government and constitution are expected, and will certainly occur. Since the legislative corps has completed the Napoleon code of civil and criminal justice, it is considered by the Emperor not only as useless, but troublesome and superfluous. For the same reasons the tribunate will also be laid aside, and His Majesty will rule the French empire, with the assistance of his senate, and with the advice of his council of state, exclusively. You know that the senators, as well as the councillors of state, are nominated by the Emperor; that he changes the latter according to his whim, and that though the former, according to the present constitution, are to hold their offices for life, the alterations which remove entirely the legislature and the tribunate may also make senators movable. But as all members of the senate are favourites or relatives, he will probably not think it necessary to resort to such a measure of *policy*.

In a former letter I have already mentioned the heterogeneous composition of the senate. The tribunate and legislative corps are worthy to figure by its side; their members are also *ci-devant* mechanics of all descriptions, debased attorneys or apostate priests, national spoilers or rebellious regicides, degraded nobles or dishonoured officers. The nearly unanimous vote of these corps for a consulate for life, and for an hereditary Emperor, cannot, therefore, either be expressive of the national will, or constitute the legality of Bonaparte's sovereignty.

In the legislature no vote opposed, and no voice declaimed against, Bonaparte's imperial dignity; but in the tribunate, Carnot — the infamously notorious Carnot — *pro formâ*, and with the permission of the Emperor *in petto*, spoke against the return of a monarchical form of government. This farce of deception and roguery did not impose even on our *good* Parisians, otherwise, and so frequently, the dupes of all our political and revolutionary mountebanks. Had Carnot expressed a sentiment or used a word not previously approved by Bonaparte, instead of reposing himself in the tribunate, he would have been wandering in Cayenne.

Son of an obscure attorney at Nolay, in Burgundy, he was brought up, like Bonaparte in one of those military schools established by the munificence of the French monarchs ; and had obtained, from the late King, the commission of a captain of engineers when the Revolution broke out. He was particularly indebted to the Prince of Condé for his support during the earlier part of his life, and yet he joined the enemies of his House, and voted for the death of Louis XVI. A member, with Robespierre and Barrère, of the Committee of Public Safety, he partook of their power, as well as of their crimes, though he has been audacious enough to deny that he had anything to do with other transactions than those of the armies. Were no other proofs to the contrary collected, a letter of his own hand to the ferocious Lebon, at Arras, is a written evidence which he is unable to refute. It is dated November 16th, 1793. "You must take," says he, "in your energy, all measures of terror commanded or required by present circumstances. Continue your revolutionary attitude ; never mind the amnesty pronounced with the acceptance of the absurd constitution of 1791 ; it is a crime which cannot extenuate other crimes. Anti-republicans can only expiate their folly under the axe of the guillotine. The public treasury will always pay the journeys and expenses of informers, because they have deserved well of their country. Let all suspected traitors expire by the sword or by fire ; continue to march upon that revolutionary line so well delineated by you. The committee applauds all your undertakings, all your measures of vigour; they are not only all permitted, but commanded by your mission."—Most of the decrees concerning the establishment of revolutionary tribunals, and particularly that for the organization of the atrocious military commission at Orange, were signed by him.

Carnot, as an officer of engineers, certainly is not without talents; but his presumption in declaring himself the sole author of those plans of campaign, which, during the years 1794, 1795 and 1796, were so triumphantly executed by Pichegru, Moreau and Bonaparte, is impertinent, as well as unfounded. At the risk of his own life, Pichegru entirely altered the plan sent him by the Committee of Public Safety; and it was Moreau's masterly retreat, which no plan of campaign could prescribe, that made this general so famous. The surprising successes of Bonaparte in Italy were both unexpected and unforeseen by the Directory; and, according to Berthier's assertion, obliged the commander-in-chief, during the first four months, to change five times his plans of proceedings and undertakings.

During his temporary sovereignty as a director, Carnot *honestly* has made a fortune of twelve millions of livres— £500,000; which has enabled him not only to live in style with his wife, but also to keep in style two sisters, of the name of Aublin, as his mistresses. He was the *friend* of the father of these girls, and promised him when condemned to the guillotine in 1793, to be their second father; but he debauched and ruined them both before either was fourteen years of age: and young Aublin, who, in 1796, reproached him with the infamy of his conduct, was delivered up by him to a military commission, which condemned him to be shot as an emigrant. He has two children by each of these unfortunate girls.

Bonaparte employs Carnot, but despises and mistrusts him; being well aware that, should another National Convention be convoked and the Emperor of the French be arraigned, as the King of France was, he would, with as great pleasure, vote for the execution of Napoleon the First as he did for that of Louis XVI. He has waded too far in blood and crime to retrograde.

To this sample of a modern tribune I will add a specimen of a modern legislator. Baptiste Cavaignac was, before the Revolution, an excise officer, turned out of his place for infidelity; but the department of Lot electing him, in 1792, a representative of the people to the National Convention, he there voted for the death of Louis XVI. and remained a faithful associate of Marat and Robespierre. After the evacuation of Verdun by the Prussians, in October, 1792, he made a report to the Convention, according to which eighty-four citizens of that town were arrested and executed. Among these were twenty-two young girls, under twenty years of age, whose crime was the having presented nosegays to the late King of Prussia on his entry after the surrender of Verdun. He was afterwards a national commissary with the armies on the coast near Brest, on the Rhine and in the Western Pyrenées, and everywhere he signalized himself by unheard-of ferocities and sanguinary deeds. The following anecdote, printed and published by our revolutionary annalist, Prudhomme, will give you some idea of the morality of this our regenerator and Imperial Solon: "Cavaignac and another deputy, Pinet," writes Prudhomme, "had ordered a box to be kept for them at the play-house at Bayonne on the evening they expected to arrive in that town. Entering very late, they found two soldiers, who had seen the box empty, placed in its front. These they ordered immediately to be arrested, and condemned them for having *outraged* the national representation, to be guillotined on the next day, when they both were accordingly executed!" Labarrère, a provost of the Maréchaussée at Dax, was in prison as a suspected person. His daughter, a very handsome girl of seventeen, lived with an aunt at St. Sévère. The two pro-consuls passing through that place, she threw herself at their feet, imploring mercy for her parent. This they not only promised, but offered her a place in their carriage to Dax, that she might see him restored to liberty. On the road the monsters insisted on a ransom for the blood of her father. Waiting, afflicted and ashamed, at a friend's house at Dax, the accomplishment of a promise so dearly purchased, she heard the beating of the alarm drum, and looked, from curiosity, through the window, when she saw her unfortunate parent ascending the scaffold! After having remained lifeless for half-an-hour, she recovered her senses an instant, when she exclaimed, "Oh, the barbarians! they violated me while flattering me with the hope of saving my father!" and then expired. In October, 1795, Cavaignac assisted Barras and Bonaparte in the destruction of some thousands of men, women and children in the streets of this capital, and was, therefore, in 1796, made by the Directory an inspector-general of the customs; and, in 1803, nominated by Bonaparte a legislator. His colleague, Citizen Pinet, is now one of our Emperor's counsellors of state, and both are commanders of His Majesty's Legion of Honour: rich, *respected* and *frequented* by our most fashionable *ladies* and *gentlemen*.

LETTER LXXIII

Paris, *October*, 1805.

My Lord,—I suppose your Government too vigilant and too patriotic not to be informed of the great and uninterrupted activity which reigns in our arsenals, dockyards and sea-ports. I have seen a plan according to which Bonaparte is enabled, and intends, to build twenty ships of the line and ten frigates, besides cutters, *in the year*, for ten years to come. I read the calculation of the expenses, the names of the forests where the timber is to be cut, of the foreign countries where a part of the necessary materials are already engaged, and of our own departments which are to furnish the remainder. The whole has been drawn up in a precise and clear manner by Bonaparte's maritime prefect at Antwerp, M. Malouet, well known in your country, where he long remained as an emigrant, and, I believe, was even employed by your ministers.

You may, perhaps, smile at this vast naval scheme of Bonaparte; but if you consider that he is the master of all the forests, mines, and productions of France, Italy, and of a great part of Germany, with all the navigable rivers and sea-ports of these countries and Holland, and remember also the character of the man, you will, perhaps, think it less impracticable. The greatest obstacle he has to encounter, and to remove, is want of experienced naval officers, though even in this he has advanced greatly since the present war, during which he has added to his naval forces twenty-nine ships of the line, thirty-four frigates, twenty-one cutters, three thousand prams, gunboats, pinnaces, &c., with four thousand naval officers and thirty-seven thousand sailors, according to the same account, signed by Malouet. It is true that most of our new naval heroes have never ventured far from our coast, and all their naval laurels have been gathered under our land batteries; but the impulse is given to the national spirit, and our conscripts in the maritime departments prefer, to a man, the navy to the army, which was not formerly the case.

It cannot have escaped your observation that the incorporation of Genoa procured us, in the South of our empire, a naval station and arsenal, as a counterpoise to Antwerp, our new naval station in the North, where twelve ships of the line have been built, or are building, since 1803, and where timber and other materials are collected for eight more. At Genoa, two ships of the line and four frigates have lately been launched, and four ships and two frigates are on the stocks; and the Genoese Republic has added sixteen thousand seafaring men to our navy. Should Bonaparte terminate successfully the present war, Naples and Venice will increase the number of our sea-ports and resources on the borders of the Mediterranean and Adriatic Seas. All his courtiers say that he will conquer Italy in Germany, and determine at Vienna the fate of London.

Of all our admirals, however, we have not one to compare with your Nelson, your Hood, your St. Vincent and your Cornwallis. By the appointment of Murat as grand admiral, Bonaparte seems to indicate that he is inclined to imitate the example of Louis XVI., in the beginning of his reign, and entrust the chief command of his fleets and squadrons to military men of approved capacity and courage, officers of his land troops. Last June, when he expected a probable junction of the fleet under Villeneuve with the squadron under Admiral Winter, and the union of both with Ganteaume at Brest, Murat was to have had the chief command of the united French, Spanish and Batavian fleets, and to support the landing of our troops in your country; but the arrival of Lord Nelson in the West Indies, and the victory of Admiral Calder, deranged all our plans and postponed all our designs, which the Continental war has interrupted; to be commenced, God knows when.

The best amongst our bad admirals is certainly Truguet; but he was disgraced last year, and exiled twenty leagues from the coast, for having declared too publicly "that our flotillas would never be serviceable before our fleets were superior to yours, *when they would become useless.*" An intriguer by long habit and by character, having neither property nor principles, he joined the Revolution, and was the second in command under Latouche, in the first republican fleet that left our harbours. He directed the expedition against Sardinia, in January, 1793, during which he acquired neither honour nor glory, being repulsed with great loss by the inhabitants. After being imprisoned under Robespierre, the Directory made him a minister of the marine, an ambassador to Spain, and a vice-admiral of France. In this capacity he commanded at Brest, during the first eighteen months of the present war. He has an irreconcilable foe in Talleyrand, with whom he quarrelled, when on his embassy in Spain, about some extortions at Madrid, which he declined to share with his principal at Paris. Such was our minister's inveteracy against him in 1798, that a directorial decree placed him on the list of emigrants, because he remained in Spain after having been recalled to France. In 1799, during Talleyrand's disgrace, Truguet returned here, and, after in vain challenging his enemy to fight, caned him in the Luxembourg gardens, a chastisement which our premier bore with true Christian patience. Truguet is not even a member of the Legion of Honour.

Villeneuve is supposed not much inferior in talents, experience and *modesty* to Truguet. He was, before the Revolution, a lieutenant of the royal navy; but his principles did not prevent him from deserting to the colours of the enemies of royalty, who promoted him first to a captain and afterwards to an admiral. His first command as such was over a division of the Toulon fleet, which, in the winter of 1797, entered Brest. In the battle at Aboukir he was the second in command; and, after the death of Admiral Brueys, he rallied the ships which had escaped, and sailed for Malta, where, two years afterwards, he signed, with General Vaubois, the capitulation of that island. When hostilities again broke out, he commanded in the West Indies, and, leaving his station, escaped your cruisers, and was appointed first to the chief command of the Rochefort, and afterwards of the Toulon fleet, on the death of Admiral Latouche. Notwithstanding the gasconade of his report of his negative victory over Admiral Calder, Villeneuve is not a Gascon by birth, but only by sentiment.

Ganteaume does not possess either the intriguing character of Truguet or the *valorous* one of Villeneuve. Before the Revolution he was a mate of a merchantman, but when most of the officers of the former royal navy had emigrated or perished, he was, in 1793, made a captain of the republican navy, and in 1796 an admiral. During the battle of Aboukir he was the chief of the staff, under Admiral Brueys, and saved himself by swimming, when *l'Orient* took fire and blew up. Bonaparte wrote to him on this occasion: . "The picture you have sent me of the disaster of *l'Orient*, and of your own dreadful situation, is horrible; but be assured that, having such a miraculous escape, DESTINY intends you to avenge one day our navy and our friends." This note was written in August, 1798, shortly after Bonaparte had professed himself a Mussulman.

When, in the summer of 1799, our general-in-chief had determined to leave his army of Egypt to its *destiny*, Ganteaume equipped and commanded the squadron of frigates which brought him to Europe, and was, after his consulate, appointed a counsellor of state and commander at Brest. In 1800 he escaped with a division of the Brest fleet to Toulon, and, in the summer of 1801, when he was ordered to carry succours to Egypt, your ship, *Swiftsure* fell in with him and was captured. As he did not, however, succeed in landing in Egypt the troops on board his ships, a temporary disgrace was incurred, and he was deprived of the command, but made a maritime prefect. Last year favour was restored him, with the command of our naval forces at Brest. All officers who have served under Ganteaume agree that, let his fleet be ever so superior, he will never fight if he can avoid it, and that, in orderly times, his *capacity* would, at the utmost, make him regarded as a good master of a merchantman, and nothing else.

Of the present commander of our flotilla at Boulogne, Lacrosse, I will also say some few words. A lieutenant before the Revolution, he became, in 1789, one of the most ardent and violent Jacobins, and in 1792 was employed by the *friend of the Blacks*, and our minister, Monge, as an emissary in the West Indies, to preach there to the negroes the rights of man and insurrection against the whites, their masters. In 1800, Bonaparte advanced him to a captain-general at Guadeloupe, an island which his plots, eight years before, had involved in all the horrors of anarchy, and where, when he now attempted to restore order, his former instruments rose against him and forced him to escape to one of your islands — I believe Dominico. Of this island, in return for his hospitable reception, he took plans, according to which our General Lagrange endeavoured to conquer it last spring. Lacrosse is a perfect revolutionary fanatic, unprincipled, cruel, unfeeling and intolerant. His presumption is great, but his talents are trifling.

LETTER LXXIV

Paris, *October*, 1805.

My Lord,— The defeat of the Austrians has excited great satisfaction among our courtiers and public functionaries; but the mass of the inhabitants here are too miserable to feel for anything else but their own sufferings. They know very well that every victory rivets their fetters, that no disasters can make them more heavy, and no triumph lighter. Totally indifferent about external occurrences, as well as about internal oppressions, they strive to forget both the past and the present, and to be indifferent as to the future; they would be glad could they cease to feel that they exist. The police officers were now, with their gendarmes, bayoneting them into illuminations for Bonaparte's successes, as they dragooned them last year into rejoicings for his coronation. I never observed before so much apathy; and in more than one place I heard the people say, "Oh! how much better we should be with fewer victories and more tranquillity, with less splendour and more security, with an honest peace instead of a brilliant war." But in a country groaning under a military government, the opinions of the people are counted for nothing.

At Madame Joseph Bonaparte's circle, however, the countenances were not so gloomy. There a real or affected joy seemed to enliven the usual dulness of these parties; some actors were repeating patriotic verses in honour of the victor; while others were singing airs or vaudevilles, to inspire our warriors with as much hatred towards your nation as gratitude towards our Emperor. It is certainly neither *philosophical* nor *philanthropical* not to exclude the vilest of all passions, HATRED, on such a *happy* occasion. Martin, in the dress of a conscript, sang six long couplets against the tyrants of the seas; of which I was only able to retain the following one:—

> Je *déteste* le peuple anglais,
> Je *déteste* son ministère;
> J'aime l'Empereur des Français,
> J'aime la paix, je hais la guerre;
> Mais puisqu'il faut la soutenir
> Contre une *Nation Sauvage*,
> Mon plus doux, mon plus grand désir
> Est de montrer tout mon courage.

But what arrested my attention, more than anything else which occurred in this circle on that evening, was a printed paper mysteriously handed about, and of which, thanks to the civility of a counsellor of state, I at last got a sight. It was a list of those persons, of different countries, whom the Emperor of the French has *fixed* upon, to *replace all the ancient dynasties of Europe within twenty years to come*. From the names of these individuals, some of whom are known to me, I could perceive that Bonaparte had more difficulty to select proper Emperors, Kings and Electors, than he would have had, some years ago, to choose directors or consuls. Our inconsistency is, however, evident even here; I did not read a name that is not found in the annals of Jacobinism and republicanism. We have, at the same time, taken care not to forget ourselves in this new distribution of supremacy. France is to furnish the stock of the new dynasties for Austria, England, Spain, Denmark and Sweden. What would you think, were you to awake one morning the subject of King Arthur O'Connor the First? You would, I dare say, be even more surprised than I am in being the subject of Napoleon Bonaparte the First. You know, I suppose, that O'Connor is a general of division, and a commander of the Legion of Honour; the bosom friend of Talleyrand, and courting, at this moment, a young lady, a relation of our Empress, whose portion may one day be an empire. But I am told that, notwithstanding Talleyrand's recommendations, and the approbation of Her Majesty, the lady prefers a colonel, her own countryman, to the Irish general. Should, however, our Emperor announce his determination, she would be obliged to marry as he commands, were he even to give her his groom, or his horse, for a spouse.

You can form no idea how wretched and despised all the Irish rebels are here. O'Connor alone is an exception: and this he owes to Talleyrand, to General Valence and to Madame de Genlis; but even he is looked on with a sneer, and, if he ever was respected in England, must endure with poignancy the contempt to which he is frequently exposed in France. When I was in your country I often heard it said that the Irish were generally considered as a debased and perfidious people, extremely addicted to profligacy and drunkenness, and, when once drunk, more cruelly ferocious than even our Jacobins. I thought it then, and I still believe it, a national prejudice, because I am convinced that the vices or virtues of all civilized nations are relatively the same; but those Irish rebels we have seen here, and who must be, like our Jacobins, the very dregs of their country, have conducted themselves so as to inspire not only mistrust but abhorrence. It is also an undeniable truth that they were greatly disappointed by our former and present government. They expected to enjoy liberty and equality, and a *pension* for their treachery; but our police commissaries caught them at their landing, our gendarmes escorted them as criminals to their place of destination, and there they received just enough to prevent them from starving. If they complained they were put in irons, and if they attempted to escape they were sent to the galleys as malefactors or shot as spies. Despair, therefore, no doubt induced many to perpetrate acts of which they were accused, and to rob, swindle and murder, because they were punished as thieves and assassins. But some of them, who have been treated in the most friendly, hospitable, and generous manner in this capital, have proved themselves ungrateful, as well as infamous. A lady of my acquaintance, of a once large fortune, had nothing left but some furniture, and her subsistence depended upon what she got by letting furnished lodgings. Mischance brought three young Irishmen to her house, who pretended to be in daily expectation of remittances from their country, and of a pension from Bonaparte. During six months she not only lodged and supported them, but embarrassed herself to procure them linen and a decent apparel. At last she was informed that each of them had been allowed sixty livres—£2 10s.- in the month, and that arrears had been paid them for nine months. Their debt to her was above three thousand livres—£125—but the day after she asked for payment they decamped, and one of them persuaded her daughter, a girl of fourteen, to elope with him and to assist him in robbing her mother of all her plate. He has, indeed, been since arrested and sentenced to the galleys for eight years; but this punishment neither restored the daughter her virtue nor the mother her property. The other two denied their debts, and, as she had no other evidence but her own scraps of accounts, they could not be forced to pay; their obdurate effrontery and infamy, however, excited such an indignation in the judges, that they delivered them over as swindlers to the *Tribunal Correctional;* and the minister of police ordered them to be transported as rogues and vagabonds to the colonies. The daughter died shortly after, in consequence of a miscarriage, and the mother did not survive her more than a month, and ended her days in the Hôtel Dieu, one of our common hospitals. Thus, these depraved young men ruined and murdered their benefactress and her child; and displayed, before they were thirty, such a consummate villainy as few wretches grown hoary in vice have perpetrated. This act of scandalous notoriety injured the Irish reputation very much in this country; for here, as in many other places, inconsiderate people are apt to judge a whole nation according to the behaviour of some few of its outcasts.

LETTER LXXV

Paris, *October*, 1805.

My Lord,—The plan of the campaign of the Austrians is incomprehensible to all our military men—not on account of its profundity, but on account of its absurdity or incoherency. In the present circumstances, half-measures must always be destructive, and it is better to strike strongly and firmly than justly. To invade Bavaria without disarming the Bavarian army, and to enter Suabia and yet acknowledge the neutrality of Switzerland, are such political and military errors as require long successes to repair, but which such an enemy as Bonaparte always takes care not to leave unpunished.

The long inactivity of the army under the Archduke Charles has as much surprised us as the defeat of the army under General von Mack; but from what I know of the former, I am persuaded that he would long since have pushed forward had not his movements been unfortunately combined with those of the latter. The House of Lorraine never produced a more valiant warrior, nor Austria a more liberal or better instructed statesman, than this Prince. Heir to the talents of his ancestors, he has commanded with glory against France during the revolutionary war ; and, although he sometimes experienced defeats, he has rendered invaluable services to the chief of his House by his courage, by his activity, by his constancy, and by that salutary firmness which, in calling the generals and superior officers to their duty, has often reanimated the confidence and the ardour of the soldier.

The Archduke Charles began, in 1793, his military career under the Prince of Coburg, the commander-in-chief of the Austrian armies in Brabant, where he commanded the advanced guard, and distinguished himself by a valour sometimes bordering on temerity, but which by degrees acquired him that esteem and popularity among the troops often very advantageous to him afterwards. He was, in 1794, appointed governor and captain-general of the Low Countries, and a field-marshal lieutenant of the army of the German empire. In April, 1796, he took the command-in-chief of the armies of Austria and of the empire, and, in the following June, engaged in several combats with General Moreau, in which he was repulsed, but in a manner that did equal honour to the victor and to the vanquished.

The Austrian army on the Lower Rhine, under General Wartensleben, having, about this time, been nearly dispersed by General Jourdan, the Archduke left some divisions of his forces under General Latour, to impede the progress of Moreau, and went with the remainder into Franconia, where he defeated Jourdan near Amberg and Wurzburg, routed his army entirely, and forced him to repass the Rhine in the greatest confusion, and with immense loss. The retreat of Moreau was the consequence of the victories of this Prince. After the capture of Kehl, in January, 1797, he assumed the command of the army of Italy, where he in vain employed all his efforts to put a stop to the victorious progress of Bonaparte, with whom at last he signed the preliminaries of peace at Leoben. In the spring of 1799, he again defeated Jourdan in Suabia, as he had done two years before in Franconia; but in Switzerland he met with an abler adversary in General Massena: still, I am inclined to think that he displayed there more real talents than anywhere else; and that this part of his campaign of 1799 was the most interesting, in a military point of view.

The most implacable enemies of the politics of the House of Austria render justice to the plans, to the frankness, to the morality of Archduke Charles: and, what is remarkable, of all the chiefs who have commanded against revolutionary France, he alone has seized the true manner of combating enthusiasts or slaves: at least, his proclamations are the only ones composed with adroitness, and are what they ought to be, because in them an appeal is made to the public opinion at a time when opinion almost constitutes half the strength of armies.

The present opposer of this Prince in Italy is one of our best, as well as most fortunate, generals. A Sardinian subject, and a deserter from the Sardinian troops, he assisted, in 1792, our commander, General Anselm, in the conquest of the county of Nice, rather as a spy than as a soldier. His knowledge of the Maritime Alps obtained, in 1793, a place on our staff, where, from the services he rendered, the rank of a general of brigade was soon conferred on him. In 1796 he was promoted to serve as a general of division under Bonaparte in Italy, where he distinguished himself so much that when, in 1798, General Berthier was ordered to accompany the army of the East to Egypt, he succeeded him as commander-in-chief of our troops in the temporary Roman Republic. But his merciless pillage, and, perhaps, the idea of his being a foreigner, brought on a mutiny, and the Directory was obliged to recall him. It was his campaign in Switzerland of 1799, and his defence of Genoa in 1800, that principally ranked him high as a military chief. After the battle of Marengo, he received the command of the army of Italy; but his extortions produced a revolt among the inhabitants, and he lived for some time in retreat and disgrace, after a violent quarrel with Bonaparte, during which many severe truths were said and heard on both sides.

After the Peace of Luneville, he seemed inclined to join Moreau, and other discontented generals: but observing, no doubt, their want of views and union, he retired to an estate he has bought near Paris, where Bonaparte visited him, after the rupture with your country, and made him, we may conclude, such offers as tempted him to leave his retreat. Last year he was nominated one of our Emperor's field-marshals, and as such he relieved Jourdan of the command in the kingdom of Italy. He has purchased *with a part* of his spoil, for fifteen millions of livres—£625,000—property, in France and Italy: and is considered worth double that sum in jewels, money and other valuables.

Massena is called, in France, *the spoiled child of fortune:* and as Bonaparte, like our former Cardinal Mazarin, has more confidence in fortune than in merit, he is, perhaps, more indebted to the former than to the latter for his present situation; his familiarity has made him disliked at our Imperial Court, where he never addresses Napoleon and Madame Bonaparte as an Emperor or an Empress without smiling.

General St. Cyr, our second in command of the army

of Italy, is also an officer of great talents and distinction. He was, in 1791, only a cornet, but, in 1795, he headed, as a general, a division of the army of the Rhine. In his report to the Directory, during the famous retreat of 1796, Moreau speaks highly of this general, and admits that his achievements, in part, saved the republican army. During 1799 he served in Italy, and in 1800 he commanded the centre of the army of the Rhine, and assisted in gaining the victory of Hohenlinden. After the Peace of Luneville, he was appointed a counsellor of state of the military section, a place he still occupies, notwithstanding his present employment. Though under forty years of age, he is rather infirm, from the fatigues he has undergone and the wounds he has received. Although he has never combated as a general-in-chief, there is no doubt but that he would fill such a place with honour to himself and advantage to his country.

Of the general officers who command under Archduke Charles, Count de Bellegarde is already known by his exploits during the last war. He had distinguished himself already in 1793, particularly when Valenciennes and Maubeuge were besieged by the united Austrian and English forces; and, in 1794, he commanded the column at the head of which the Emperor marched, when Landrecy was invested. In 1796, he was one of the members of the council of the Archduke Charles, when this Prince commanded for the first time as a general-in-chief, on which occasion he was promoted to a field-marshal lieutenant. He displayed again great talents during the campaign of 1799, when he headed a small corps, placed between General Suwarow in Italy, and Archduke Charles in Switzerland ; and in this delicate post he contributed equally to the success of both. After the Peace of Luneville he was appointed a commander-in-chief for the Emperor in the *ci-devant* Venetian States, where the troops composing the army under the Archduke Charles were, last summer, received and inspected by him, before the arrival of the Prince. He is considered by military men as greatly superior to most of the generals now employed by the Emperor of Germany.

LETTER LXXVI

PARIS, *October*, 1805.

MY LORD,—" I would give my *brother*, the Emperor of Germany, one further piece of advice. Let him hasten to make peace. *This is the crisis* when, he must recollect, all States must have an end. *The idea of the approaching extinction of the dynasty of Lorraine must impress him with horror.*" When Bonaparte ordered this paragraph to be inserted in the *Moniteur*, he discovered an *arrière pensée*, long suspected by politicians, but never before avowed by himself, or by his ministers. "That he has determined on the universal change of dynasties, because a usurper can never reign with safety or *honour* as long as any legitimate prince may disturb his power, or reproach him for his rank." Elevated with prosperity, or infatuated with vanity and pride, he spoke a language which his placemen, courtiers, and even his brother Joseph, at first thought *premature*, if not indiscreet. If all lawful sovereigns do not read in these words their proscription, and the fate which the most powerful usurper that ever desolated mankind has destined for them, it may be ascribed to that blindness with which Providence, in its wrath, sometimes strikes those doomed to be grand examples of the vicissitudes of human life.

"Had Talleyrand," said Louis Bonaparte, in his wife's drawing-room, "been by my brother's side, he would not have unnecessarily alarmed or awakened those whom it should have been his policy to keep in a soft slumber, until his blows had laid them down to rise no more; but his soldier-like *frankness* frequently injures his political views." This I *myself heard* Louis say to Abbé Siéyes, though several foreign ambassadors were in the saloon, near enough not to miss a word. If it was really meant as a reflection on Napoleon, it was imprudent; if designed as a defiance to other princes, it was unbecoming and impertinent. I am inclined to believe it, considering the individual to whom it was addressed, a premeditated declaration that our Emperor expected a universal war, was prepared for it, and was certain of its fortunate issue.

When this Siéyes is often consulted, and publicly flattered, our politicians say, "Woe to the happiness of sovereigns and to the tranquillity of subjects; the fiend of mankind is busy, and at work," and, in fact, ever since 1789, the infamous ex-abbé has figured, either as a plotter or as an actor, in all our dreadful and sanguinary revolutionary epochas. The accomplice of La Fayette in 1789, of Brissot in 1791, of Marat in 1792, of Robespierre in 1793, of Tallien in 1794, of Barras in 1795, of Rewbel in 1797, and of Bonaparte in 1799, he has hitherto planned, served, betrayed or deserted all factions. He is one of the few of our grand criminals, who, after enticing and sacrificing his associates, has been fortunate enough to survive them. Bonaparte has heaped upon him presents, places and pensions; national property, senatories, knighthoods and palaces; but he is, nevertheless, not supposed one of our Emperor's most dutiful subjects, because many of the late changes have differed from his metaphysical schemes of innovation, of regeneration, and of overthrow. He has too high an opinion of his own deserts not to consider it beneath his philosophical dignity to be a contented subject of a fellow-subject, elevated into supremacy by his labours and dangers. His *modesty* has, for these sixteen years past, ascribed to his talents all the *glory* and *prosperity* of France, and all her misery and misfortunes to the disregard of his counsels, and to the neglect of his advice. Bonaparte knows it; and that he is one of those crafty, sly, and dark conspirators, more dangerous than the bold assassin, who, by sophistry, art and perseverance insinuate into the minds of the unwary and daring, the ideas of their plots, in such an insidious manner that they take them and foster them as the production of their own genius; he is, therefore, watched by our imperial spies, and never consulted but when any great blow is intended to be struck, or some enormous atrocities perpetrated. A month before the seizure of the Duke of Enghien, and the murder of Pichegru, he was every day shut up for some hours with Napoleon Bonaparte at St. Cloud, or in the Tuileries; where he has hardly been seen since, except after our Emperor's return from his coronation as a King of Italy.

Siéyes never was a republican, and it was cowardice alone that made him vote for the death of his King and benefactor: although he is very fond of his own metaphysical notions, he always has preferred the preservation of his life to the profession or adherence to his systems. He will not think the Revolution complete, or the constitution of his country a good one, until some Napoleon, or some Louis, writes himself an Emperor or King of France, *by the grace of Siéyes*. He would expose the lives of thousands to obtain such a compliment to his hateful vanity and excessive pride; but he would not take a step that endangered his personal safety, though it might eventually lead him to the possession of a crown.

From the bounty of his King, Siéyes had, before the Revolution, an income of fifteen thousand livres £625 per annum; his places, pensions and landed estates produce now yearly five hundred thousand livres £20,000—not including the interest of his money in the French and foreign funds. Two years ago he was exiled, for some time, to an estate of his in Touraine, and Bonaparte even deliberated about transporting him to Cayenne, when Talleyrand observed, "that such a condemnation would endanger that colony of France, as he would certainly organize there a focus of revolutions, which might also involve Surinam and the Brazils, the colonies of our allies, in one common ruin. In the present circumstances," added the minister, "if Siéyes is to be transported, I wish we could land him in England, Scotland or Ireland, or even in Russia."

I have just heard from a general officer the following anecdote, which he read to me from a letter of another general, dated Ulm, the 25th instant, and, if true, it explains in part Bonaparte's apparent indiscretion in the threat thrown out against all ancient dynasties.

Among his confidential generals (and hitherto the most irreproachable of all our military commanders), Marmont is particularly distinguished. Before Napoleon left this capital to head his armies in Germany, he is stated to have sent despatches to all those traitors dispersed in different countries whom he has selected to commence the new dynasties, under the *protection* of the Bonaparte Dynasty. They were, no doubt, advised of *this being the crisis* when they had to begin their machinations against thrones. A courier from Talleyrand at Strasburg to Bonaparte at Ulm was ordered to pass by the corps under the command of Marmont, to whom, in case the Emperor had advanced too far into Germany, he was to deliver his papers. This courier was surprised and interrupted by some Austrian light troops; and, as it was only some few hours after being informed of this capture that Bonaparte expressed himself frankly, as related above, it was supposed by his army that the Austrian Government had already in its power despatches which made our schemes of *improvement* at Paris no longer any secrets at Vienna. The writer of this letter added that General Marmont was highly distressed on account of this accident, which might retard the prospect of restoring to Europe its long lost peace and tranquillity.

This officer made his first campaign under Pichegru in 1794, and was, in 1796, appointed by Bonaparte one of his aides-de-camp. His education had been entirely military, and in the practice the war afforded him he soon evinced how well he remembered the lessons of theory. In the year 1796, at the battle of Saint-Georges, before Mantua, he charged at the head of the eighth battalion of grenadiers, and contributed much to its fortunate issue. In October of the same year, Bonaparte, as a mark of his satisfaction, sent him to present to the Directory the numerous colours which the army of Italy had conquered; from whom he received in return a pair of pistols, with a fraternal hug from Carnot. On his return to Italy he was, for the first time, employed by his chief in a political capacity. A republic, and nothing but a republic, being then the order of the day, some Italian patriots were convoked at Reggio to arrange a plan for a Cisalpine Republic, and for the incorporation with it of Modena, Bologna and other neutral states; Marmont was nominated a French republican plenipotentiary, and assisted as such in the organization of a commonwealth, which since has been by turns a province of Austria or a tributary state of France.

Marmont, though combating for a bad cause, is an honest man; his hands are neither soiled with plunder, nor stained with blood. Bonaparte, among his other *good* qualities, wishes to see everyone about him rich; and those who have been too delicate to accumulate wealth by pillage, he generally provides for, by putting into requisition some great heiress. After the Peace of Campo Formio, Bonaparte arrived at Paris, where he demanded in marriage for his aide-de-camp Marmont, Mademoiselle Perregeaux, the sole child of the first banker in France, a well-educated and accomplished young lady, who would be much more agreeable did not her continual smiles and laughing indicate a degree of self-satisfaction and complacency which may be felt, but ought never to be published.

The banker, Perregeaux, is one of those fortunate beings who, by drudgery and assiduity, has succeeded in some few years to make an ample fortune. A Swiss by birth, like Necker, he also, like him, after gratifying the passion of avidity, showed an ambition to shine in other places than in the counting-house and upon the exchange. Under La Fayette, in 1790, he was the chief of a battalion of the Parisian National Guards; under Robespierre, a commissioner for purchasing provisions; and under Bonaparte he is become a senator and a commander of the Legion of Honour. I am *told* that he has made all his money by his connections with your country; but I *know* that the favourite of Napoleon can never be the friend of Great Britain. He is a widower; but Mademoiselle Mars, of the Emperor's theatre, consoles him for the loss of his wife.

General Marmont accompanied Bonaparte to Egypt, and distinguished himself at the capture of Malta, and when, in the following year, the siege of St. Jean d'Acre was undertaken, he was ordered to extend the fortifications of Alexandria; and if, in 1801, they retarded your progress, it was owing to his abilities, being an officer of engineers as well as of the artillery. He returned with Bonaparte to Europe, and was, after his usurpation, made a counsellor of state. At the battle of Marengo he commanded the artillery, and signed afterwards, with the Austrian general, Count Hohenzollern, the Armistice of Treviso, which preceded shortly the Peace of Luneville. Nothing has abated Bonaparte's attachment to this officer, whom he appointed a commander-in-chief in Holland, when a change of government was intended there, and whom he will entrust everywhere else, where sovereignty is to be abolished, or thrones and dynasties subverted.

LETTER LXXVII

Paris, October, 1805.

My Lord,—Many wise people are of opinion that the revolution of another great empire is necessary to combat or oppose the great impulse occasioned by the Revolution of France, before Europe can recover its long-lost order and repose. Had the subjects of Austria been as disaffected as they are loyal, the world might have witnessed such a terrible event, and been enabled to judge whether the hypothesis was the production of an ingenious schemer or of a profound statesman. Our armies under Bonaparte have never before penetrated into the heart of a country where subversion was not prepared, and where subversion did not follow.

How relatively insignificant, in the eyes of Providence, must be the independence of states and the liberties of nations, when such a relatively insignificant personage as General von Mack can shake them? Have, then, the Austrian heroes — a Prince Eugène, a Laudon, a Lasci, a Beaulieu, a Haddick, a Bender, a Clairfayt, and numerous other valiant and great warriors left no posterity behind them;

or has the presumption of General von Mack imposed upon the judgment of the counsellors of his Prince? This latter must have been the case; how otherwise could the welfare of their Sovereign have been entrusted to a military quack, whose want of energy and bad dispositions had, in 1799, delivered up the capital of another Sovereign to his enemies. How many reputations are gained by an impudent assurance, and lost when the man of talents is called upon to act and the fool presents himself.

Baron von Mack served as an aide-de-camp under Field-marshal Laudon, during the last war between Austria and Turkey, and displayed some intrepidity, particularly before Lissa. The Austrian army was encamped eight leagues from that place, and the commander-in-chief hesitated to attack it, believing it to be defended by thirty thousand men. To decide him upon making this attack, Baron von Mack left him at nine o'clock at night, crossed the Danube, accompanied only by a single Uhlan, and penetrated into the suburb of Lissa, where he made prisoner a Turkish officer, whom, on the next morning at seven o'clock, he presented to his general, and from whom it was learnt that the garrison contained only six thousand men. This personal temerity, and the applause of Field-marshal Laudon, procured him then a kind of reputation, which he has not since been able to support. Some theoretical knowledge of the art of war, and a great facility of conversing on military topics, made even the Emperor Joseph conceive a high opinion of this officer; but it has long been proved, and experience confirms it every day, that the difference is immense between the speculator and the operator, and that the *generals of cabinets* are often indifferent captains when in the camp or in the field.

Preceded by a certain celebrity, Baron von Mack served, in 1793, under the Prince of Coburg, as an adjutant-general, and was called to assist at the Congress at Antwerp, where the operations of the campaign were regulated. Everywhere he displayed activity and bravery; was wounded twice in the month of May; but he left the army without having performed anything that evinced the talents which fame had bestowed on him. In February, 1794, the Emperor sent him to London to arrange, in concert with your Government, the plans of the campaign then on the eve of being opened; and when he returned to the Low Countries he was advanced to a quartermaster-general of the army of Flanders, and terminated also this unfortunate campaign without having done anything to justify the reputation he had before acquired or usurped. His Sovereign continued, nevertheless, to employ him in different armies; and in January, 1797, he was appointed a field-marshal lieutenant and a quartermaster-general of the army of the

Rhine. In February he conducted fifteen thousand of the troops of this army to reinforce the army of Italy; but when Bonaparte in April penetrated into Styria and Carinthia, he was ordered to Vienna as a second in command of the levy *en masse*.

Real military characters had already formed their opinion of this officer, and saw a presumptuous charlatan where others had admired an able warrior. His own conduct soon convinced them that they neither had been rash nor mistaken. The King of Naples demanding, in 1798, from his son-in-law, the Emperor of Germany, a general to organize and head his troops, Baron von Mack was presented to him. After war had been declared against France he obtained some success in partial engagements, but was defeated in a general battle by an enemy inferior in number. In the kingdom of Naples, as well as in the empire of Germany, the fury of negotiation seized him when he should have fought, and when he should have remembered that no compacts can ever be entered into with political and military earthquakes, more than with physical ones. This imprudence, particularly as he was a foreigner, excited suspicion among his troops, whom, instead of leading to battle, he deserted, under the pretence that his life was in danger, and surrendered himself and his staff to our commander, Championnet.

A general who is *too fond* of his life ought never to enter a camp, much less to command armies; and a military chief who does not consider the happiness and honour of the State as his first passion and his first duty, and prefers existence to glory, deserves to be shot as a traitor or drummed out of the army as a dastardly coward. Without mentioning the numerous military faults committed by General von Mack during this campaign, it is impossible to deny that, with respect to his own troops, he conducted himself in the most pusillanimous manner. It has often been repeated that martial valour does not always combine with it that courage and that necessary presence of mind which knows how to direct or repress multitudes, how to command obedience and obtain popularity; but when a man is entrusted with the safety of an empire, and assumes such a brilliant situation, he must be weak-minded and despicable indeed, if he does not show himself worthy of it by endeavouring to succeed, or perish in the attempt. The French emigrant, General Dumas, evinced what might have been done, even with the dispirited Neapolitan troops, whom he neither deserted nor with whom he offered to capitulate.

Baron von Mack is in a very infirm state of health, and is often under the necessity of being carried on a litter; and his bodily complaints have certainly not increased the *vigour* of his mind. His love of life seems to augment in proportion as its real value diminishes. As to the report here of his having betrayed his trust in exchanging honour for gold, I believe it totally unfounded. Our intriguers may have deluded his understanding, but our traitors would never have been able to seduce or shake his fidelity. His head is weak, but his heart is honest. Unfortunately, it is too true that, in turbulent times, irresolution and weakness in a commander or a minister operate the same, and are as dangerous as treason.

THE END

www.ingramcontent.com/pod-product-compliance
Lightning Source LLC
Chambersburg PA
CBHW030820230426
43667CB00008B/1310